TEAM
SPIRIT

TEAM
SPIRIT

People Working with People

by
Dr David Cormack

A ministry of World Vision
MARC
EUROPE

British Library Cataloguing in Publication Data

Cormack, David
   Team Spirit.
   1. Christian leadership
   I. Title
   248.4 BV652.1

   ISBN 0-947697-55-1 (paperback)
   ISBN 0 947697 71 3 (hardback)

Unless otherwise noted, Scripture quotations in this publication are from the Holy Bible, New International Version. Copyright © 1973, 1978, 1984, International Bible Society. Published in Britain by Hodder and Stoughton. Used by permission.

MARC Europe is an integral part of World Vision, an international Christian humanitarian organisation. MARC's object is to assist Christian leaders with factual information, surveys, management skills, strategic planning and other tools for evangelism. MARC Europe also publishes and distributes related books on matters of mission, church growth, management, spiritual maturity and other topics.

Cover art: Drummond Chapman.
Cartoons: Keith Field.

Typeset for MARC Europe, 6 Homesdale Road, Bromley BR2 9EX by Furlonger Phototext Ltd, Victoria Chambers, Fir Vale Road, Bournemouth BH1 2JN and printed by Richard Clay, The Chaucer Press, Bungay, Suffolk NR35 1ED.

Contents

6

Part 5: Building on Your Experience

Introduction

Much has happened in recent years to focus attention on that all pervading social phenomenon — the human group — wishfully called 'the team'. The reasons for this interest are many. As living becomes more crowded and complex, so life becomes more stressful and involved. Even if we wish to, we cannot live in isolation. People are here to stay!

Even those who have worked in and sought to develop teams have been beset by the continuing and increasing problems of communication breakdown, individuality, and membership-change. But groups of all descriptions are in vogue — self-help groups, worship groups, project groups, etc — and more and more people are anxious to learn what can be done to enhance the life and achievement of their teams.

The benefits that come from being part of a strong group cannot be over-estimated. Membership can bring with it a sense of security, of identity and of self-worth. Within the boundaries of a supportive team you can make mistakes, be encouraged, and learn skills which will enhance your life. Some of the greatest privileges of all — those of friendship, of caring and of loving — are to be experienced in the spirit of true teamwork.

It is interesting to note that, on the one hand, people are rediscovering the value of the group, while on the other hand, Western societies are increasingly suffering from the damaging effects of individualism and isolationism. Family break-down, single-parent families, unemployment and community fragmentation are all on the increase. This is also true for the Two-Thirds World, where the traditional strengths of the human group as represented by the enlarged family and tribal or clan systems are being undermined by the drift towards the cities. As one writer has put it:

> Individualism is a novel expression, to which a novel idea has given birth. Our fathers were only acquainted with egoism (selfishness). Selfishness is a passionate and exaggerated love of self, which leads a man to connect every-

thing in the world. Individualism is a mature and calm feeling, which disposes each member of the community to sever himself from the mass of his fellows, and to draw apart with his family and his friends; so that, after he has thus formed a little circle of his own, he willingly leaves society at large to itself.[1]

Such behaviour makes it more difficult for people to form new teams or join new groups. (The terms 'team' and 'group' are used interchangeably in this text.)

The purpose of this book is that the reader might become more effective in building teams. Whether you are a leader or a member, you need to understand the skills of both membership and leadership. Throughout the book there are exercises for both team leaders and members. You should complete these as you encounter them and, where other members of your team are also working with this book, you should discuss your responses and agree on action together.

The main concern I have as I work with teams of managers or volunteers is that people look for benefits from their team without being prepared to pay the cost of team building. 'You get nowt for nowt', as they say. So it will be for you. Team building is not easy; there will be a cost, but it is rewarding.

Difficult

We are born into groups (families); we are educated in groups (classes); we play in groups (teams); we work in groups (companies); we worship in groups (congregations); we fight in groups (armies). We spend most of our waking life in groups, yet there are fewer areas of living in which we are less successful than that of living and working together. Mankind's inability to live and work in harmony confronts us on every side: internationally, we face wars and terrorism; commercially, we see the disruptive actions of employers and unions; socially − on the streets of our cities and in the hearts and minds of the inhabitants − we are dismayed by the interpersonal violence − physical, verbal or emotional.

Why should it be so difficult to create effective working relationships? What can be done to improve the performance of the teams, groups, committees, boards and families to which we belong? This book will help group leaders and members address these issues and make better use of their time, their talents and other resources in the team situation. But first some words of caution for the over-eager and some words of encouragement for the over-cautious.

The Exercise of Power

Your own interest in the subject of teams will probably be because you need to improve the operation of one or more of the teams of which you are part. Since you spend so much time in groups, any improvement will contribute significantly to your performance in life generally. However, the first point to be made is that you cannot improve the effectiveness of your group without first taking steps to improve your own performance. Team building is not about doing things *to* other people or even *for* other people; it is about doing things *with* other people.

You may be a managing director, or minister, or house-group leader, or chairman of the PTA, or Parish Council Committee, parent or partner — but whatever you are, you cannot change those with whom you work without changing how you yourself work. Team building is an activity which must be jointly owned by the team members. Team building is about changing together, and change means exercising power — the power of the team leader as he or she seeks to move the group forward; the power of experience to influence all the members, including the leader, to learn and grow and to become what they are not yet. Let us think for a few moments about the use of power as it relates to people.

Much has been written about the subject of power. In her book *The Religion of Power*, Cheryl Forbes cautions against the use of power. She reminds her readers:

> Jesus used sheep as the symbol for his people. What are sheep like? First, they are harmless. They are defenceless. They are powerless. Without the protection of the shepherd, sheep would be in constant danger from the wolves who encircle the sheep pens, wolves waiting to devour them. Jesus Christ says that he sends us out into the world as sheep, not as lions or foxes or wolves. That is how powerless we are to be.[2]

She defines power thus: 'Power means insistence on what we want, for no other reason than that we want it: it means making other people follow us despite their own wishes. Power is assumed, insensitive, dehumanising and ultimately destructive.'[3]

Power and Influence

It is clear that the exercise of such power is not going to help in team building! There is, however, another face to power. It is the power of influence. My home is in a Scottish highland valley — rocky, thin soiled and with a short growing season. The valley survives to a large extent on its sheep. In this environment the harmless, defenceless, powerless creature not only influences the lives of those more harmful and powerful than itself, but it dictates the pattern of life – lambing, shearing, dipping and feeding. Although powerless by some definitions, these sheep have considerable influence!

Professor David McClelland describes power in two forms – 'personalised' power, which is similar to that described and criticised in Cheryl Forbes' book, and 'socialised' power, which is directed at the health and well-being of others, rather than for the benefit of the individual exercising the power.[4] In this sense, Christians are 'the light of the world, and 'the salt of the earth'.[5] As such they must exercise power by words, by works and by life if they are to influence those around. Without the exercise of power, nothing can be changed. As a team builder you will require to exercise power which is directed at the well-being of others. But power is a temptation – and hence one of the dangers.

Dangers for Teams

What dangers await the would-be team builder? Here are 10 examples. More will surface as we progress, but these will do to start with! We shall examine them all in detail in the course of this study, but we need not be depressed by them; teamwork – despite all its dangers – offers the reward and the benefit of personal growth.

1 A charismatic leader may cause the team to become dependent and unable to function without the leader's presence or approval.

2 A strong team may ignore or deny the needs of others.

3 A new team may have no sense of identity, only a strong sense of purpose. It knows what it is there for, but not who it is, and may engage in hurtful activities on the assumption that the end justifies the means.

4 The changing-membership syndrome experienced by teams whose members come and go at frequent intervals, causing a loss of identity and morale.

5 Joint ventures when two or more teams try to co-operate but have different values and visions will create tension and conflict.

6 A crisis of control arises when one group gives birth to another – the 'son of team' syndrome.

7 The team may lose sight of its reason for existence and become the everlasting team.

8 Destructive conflicts and divisions within the team are always a possibility in the face of change.
9 Another group or new leader may make a surprise takeover.
10 The team may be prevented from achieving its targets by premature break-up.

Time Frame

How long does it take to build a team? I am often asked this question. Unfortunately, there is no simple answer, for it depends on the purpose of the team. Some teams are temporary — brought together for a single purpose. A good example would be a national football team in which the players come from different clubs to represent their country. To build this team, the coach may have less than one month. Teams that have a longer life can be more thorough. Management teams, for example, often stay together for three to four years. Some groups, however, may be together for life. Clearly, the time taken to build these different teams will vary according to what is required of them and according to the stability of the membership. The following quote from AD 66 shows that not much has changed in 2,000 years:

> We trained very hard, but it seemed that every time we were beginning to form up into a team, we would be reorganised. I was to learn later in life that we tended to react to any new situation by reorganising, and a wonderful method it can be for creating the illusion of progress while producing confusion, inefficiency and demoralisation.[6]

There is, however, another way to look at the time frame. *Team Spirit* provides you with material which will help your team to grow. How long will it take you to learn the skills, apply them in your team and create a strong group? This question I can answer more easily. You should allow yourself 12 to 18 months — team building is not and cannot be a superficial activity. To attempt a 'quick fix' solution to team problems will soon lead to frustration and disillusionment.

Five Stages

There are five stages involved in building a team:

- committing yourself to the process
  - acquiring the skills
  - applying the skills
- evaluating your performance
- building on your experience.

Let us look at each in detail, since these stages represent the divisions of this book and provide the foundation for what you will read in later chapters.

Commit Yourself

This is not a book about how you can improve the performance of others. Instead, it is about you and your performance in the team setting. Unless you are dissatisfied with your performance, do not proceed. But dissatisfaction is not enough, for you need to have a real desire to see change — change in yourself and in others. It is from this desire that the commitment will flow in the months ahead. What you are attempting to do is to alter your behaviour and to provide the environment in which other members of your team will wish to change their behaviour.

How you currently behave is a product of your education, experience, values and priorities. These influences are difficult to set aside, so you will not find change easy. You will therefore need commitment — an increasingly rare commodity, for people are 'suffering from a tremendous sense of loss — that numbing feeling that nothing or no one is worth being committed to.'[7] Commit yourself now to the building up of one team of which you are a member. Do not attempt to apply all the ideas to all your teams. Commit your energies initially to the development of one team.

Use the space provided opposite to list the names of the major groups, teams, and committees to which you belong.

For the remainder of this text, it is suggested that you choose to work on the development of one of the groups you have listed. Choose the team in which you would most like to see change take place. Select the team now and write its name here:

_____

Acquire the Skills

Working with people requires skills — social skills. Unfortunately, these skills are not formally considered or taught in most educational systems. We have been left to acquire them in an ad

No	Name of Team
1	
2	
3	
4	
5	
6	
7	
8	

hoc manner. Essential for good team working are the skills of listening, observation and sensitivity. Few indeed are the text-books on these critical subjects; I deal with them in Chapter 5.

A second set of skills lies in the area of team activities – what to do and when to do it. In the construction of a building, drains and foundations come first, and the roof goes on before the interior finishes are applied. So also in team building there is a sequence of activities. You will learn these in this book as we consider the team at work in Chapter 7.

Finally, at this point, I want to encourage you to think about your own gifts and skills. In a group situation, what is your main contribution? Do you lead? Do you take minutes? Are you the treasurer? Do you contribute some special knowledge? Are you there because of your position or because of your personality? Team building begins by building your own skills.

Apply the Skills

St Paul has a word of caution for those of us who love learning new theories. Looking at his own first-century world, he observed a dangerous fascination with knowledge coupled with an unwillingness to apply the learning of experience: 'always learning but never able to acknowledge the truth' was his judgement,[8] for there is nothing as useless as knowledge which is not applied.

What you learn in the course of studying this book you must apply, for only in living out the principles can you hope to make real progress in team building. This is not a theoretical book. Each chapter will require you to work through what has been presented.

Evaluate Your Performance

How do you know you are doing a good job? Whether you are a housewife, craftsman, manager, director, teacher or minister, this is an important question. For some it is obvious when our performance is poor and when it is not. For others it is less so. Peters and Waterman in their international bestseller *In Search of Excellence* attempt to identify the factors that lead to success in business. They say, 'small groups are, quite simply, the basic organisational building blocks of excellent companies . . . the small group is critical to effective organisational functioning'.[9] In a more easily read but nevertheless insightful, description of the successful manager, the writers lament how difficult the search for success was. They describe a young man who –

> . . . had looked everywhere for an effective manager but had found only a few. The few he did find would not share their secrets with him. He began to think maybe he would never find out what really made an effective manager tick.[10]

But company and business performance is perhaps easier to evaluate than the work of, say, the teacher or the minister. Recently, I have been working with an international Christian organisation which asked me to help evaluate the performance of its workers. Many of the members of the organisation were sceptical – 'How can you evaluate spiritual work? How can you evaluate education? How can you evaluate social, medical and relief work?' they asked. 'How can you evaluate teamwork?' I replied, 'I do not know yet, but if the work is important, then you must find a way of assessing your performance.' Within three months we had the pilot evaluation system in place! In this book I will provide you with ways of evaluating all that you do in the context of team building, particularly in Chapters 11 and 12.

Think for a moment of your own performance in groups – are you doing a good job? How do you know?

Build on Experience

Evaluation helps you build on experience. If you know what works well for you in group situations, you can do more of it. If you know what you do that obstructs progress, you can modify or eliminate that behaviour.

Team building is not a one-off activity. As long as the team exists, it will require maintenance. There are no 10-year guarantees with this or any other text on teamwork. Each time the team meets, the skills have to be re-applied. Nor can you transfer successful behaviour from one team and automatically have success in another — each team has its own blend of strengths and weaknesses which can be identified only after careful observation.

The First Model

We have now looked briefly at the five stages of team development:

- committing
- acquiring
- applying
- evaluating
- building.

The diagram below illustrates the fact that the five stages form a continuous process:

The Team Development Cycle

16

I will call this and similar diagrams 'models', since they provide a simple framework to represent more complex ideas and concepts.

A Final Thought
It is not an over-exaggeration to say that team building can damage your health! Do not under-estimate the effort that may be required to make real progress in some teams. As you proceed through *Team Spirit*, I will point out to you some of the pitfalls for the team builder and describe how you can reduce the effort required to make progress.

PART 1
Committing Yourself
to the Process

THE MASTER BUILDERS

Chapter 1

History and folk-lore are full of examples of successful teams — groups of men and women who, against seemingly impossible odds, won the day. Jason and the Argonauts faced a hazardous sea voyage with several monsters thrown in for good measure. Horatio held the bridge with his two companions against uncountable odds. Sir Edmund Hillary and Sherpa Tensing combined in a team of two to conquer the last few hundred feet of Mount Everest. A team of highly trained military personnel broke the Iranian Embassy siege in London while the world looked on. And every moment of every day, successful teams carry air passengers around the world.

Not all teams are successful. Captain Scott's ill-fated Antarctic expedition, although in many ways an example of outstanding team spirit, was a failure in terms of the task. The American space programme has provided the world with outstanding success and failure, while the world of sport has endless examples of surprising team performances — both good and bad.

What makes the difference between the performance of teams? Why do some teams do so well, while others fail time and time again? Clearly, it is more than a matter of the technical skill of the individuals concerned. This is demonstrated well in competitive team sports. It is also obvious in politics and government, where performance is often related to the strength of the leader rather than the quality of the team – at least in the short term. Dr Meredith Belbin studied successful teams in Britain during the late 1960s and early 1970s. He wished to identify why some teams of very able people could perform badly, while teams of quite unremarkable individuals could do well. His research showed that successful teams did not have to be made up of the best individuals around.[1] I find this encouraging because what Belbin is saying is that whoever you are, whatever your skills, you can be part of a successful team if you and the other members make the right contributions to the working of the group. In Chapters 4 and 5 I will help you identify what is needed for a group to work, as well as help you identify your own and the team's strengths and weaknesses in this important area of contribution.

Team Size

The question of how many people should be in a team is less important than most people think. The old adage 'Two's company, three's a crowd' does not really apply to teams, but we can modify it somewhat to fit: 'Two's company, three's a team, and more than fifteen's a crowd!' The optimum size appears to be seven, but the number depends entirely on the purpose of the team. Peter Robinson has produced a film called *The Secretary and Her Boss*, which examines the working relationship in a team of two.[2] Rugby shows that fifteen players can be co-ordinated well together. But there are obvious disadvantages in larger teams. Here are some:

1 difficulty in selecting people who will fit
2 the likelihood of frequent membership change
3 finding roles and tasks for each member which match their skills
4 communication between so many allows for misinterpretation
5 arranging meeting times acceptable to all
6 developing relationships (in a team of 15 there are 210 sets of one-to-one relationships!)
7 developing members' skills
8 allowing sufficient time for members to contribute
9 the dangers of sub-group formation and conflict.

What is your own experience? *Working in large teams, one problem I find is*

_____

_____

_____

Small teams, say of three or four, are ideal for some tasks and situations, but may suffer from −

1 insufficient resources
2 limited skills
3 lack of creativity
4 poor problem solving.

What is your own experience? *Working in small groups, one problem I find is*

_____

_____

_____

An Example

Perhaps the most well known and well documented team building process is that to be found in the New Testament. The Gospels give four separate descriptions of Jesus of Nazareth's approach as he selected, trained, evaluated and built a team which was to change the world. Let me suggest 10 principles for team building which can be found in his example.

First, we cannot lead others unless we know ourselves. Christ attended to his own needs as Messiah, before he began to lead others. Before he recruited the first member of his team, he confirmed his own identity. 'If you are the Son of God . . .' was his temptation.[3] Successful team building began for him by knowing who he was and knowing his relationship to God and others. As he was the Son of the Father,[4] his team members were to be family.[5] How you view yourself and the value that you place on people will influence your behaviour.

How Do You View Yourself?

How well do you know yourself? The following questionnaire is designed to help you think about your behaviour in relating to other people.

First, read over the scales and, on each one, place a circle around the number that describes your typical behaviour when you are working with other people.

A Awareness of Feelings of Others

1	2	3	4	5	6	7
Unaware						Aware

B Willingness to Confront People

1	2	3	4	5	6	7
Unwilling						Willing

C Control of Relationship

1	2	3	4	5	6	7
Always wishing to lead						Happy for others to lead

D Willingness to Change

1	2	3	4	5	6	7
Unwilling to change						Very willing to change

E Tolerance of Uncertainty

1	2	3	4	5	6	7
Low tolerance						High tolerance

F Self-confidence

1	2	3	4	5	6	7
Low confidence						High confidence

G Attitude to Conflict

1	2	3	4	5	6	7
Avoid conflict if possible						Tend to promote conflict

H Openness about Feelings

1	2	3	4	5	6	7

Reluctant to
be open about
my feelings

Willing to be open
about my feelings

I How Others See Me

1	2	3	4	5	6	7

Know how I
am seen

Don't know how
others see me

J Ability to Listen

1	2	3	4	5	6	7

Good listener

Poor listener

Now you should check your answers with someone who knows you well or, preferably, get them to complete the questionnaire for you. Pay particular attention to any aspects which your partner scores differently by two or more points on the scale. Throughout *Team Spirit* you will find ideas to develop your skills for working with people in all the above areas. Knowing yourself, then, is the first principle of team building.

Nine Other Principles

Second, we cannot lead others through the misuse of power. Christ passed the test of self-control. Before he exercised leadership over others, he exercised it over himself. He had the power to turn the stones to bread; he was hungry, but he would not use his power for his own need.[6] The team leader must be a person of self-control before he can effectively control others. It is not possible to force people to co-operate — you can only force them to submit. Leadership is the gift of those who want to be led. How is your self-control?

Third, no leader can expect to exercise authority if he is not able to submit to higher principles and orders. Christ passed the test of obedience — obedience to his Father's will and his

Father's word.[7] Unfortunately, obedience is not popular today. Hence team leaders face the problem of what I call the 'hot line to heaven' tendency, which every team member seems to exhibit when unpopular decisions are made. We all know best and claim God has told us so! The leader must be able to demonstrate his own willingness to be under authority, as an example to others.

Fourth, choose your team with care. Christ selected carefully and called with authority, 'Follow me!'[8] If you are in a position to choose a team or team member, take time to think about membership, then act decisively. Think also about what the members can become, rather than simply what they are now and what they can do now.

Fifth, do not accept anyone just to make up the numbers. Christ was prepared to state the cost of membership if there was a doubt as to a possible candidate's suitability. Because of his growing reputation, many people began to follow Jesus, and one particularly able and wealthy young man pleaded to be allowed to join the disciples. It was clear to everyone present that he would have made a good member of the team, but Christ said, 'Go, sell your possessions and give to the poor . . . Then come, follow me!' The young man's real priorities were revealed and he sadly withdrew.[9]

Sixth, team building takes time. Christ spent time with his team outside the context of the working environment. He got to know them, but more, he let them get to know him: 'he took them with him and they withdrew by themselves to a town called Bethsaida.'[10] The team that plays together, stays together. Leading a team requires a time commitment outside the team meetings. Today this principle is continued in management teams in the form of an 'away day' — a day when the team goes away, say to the country, or an hotel, or the coast.[11]

Seventh, recognise the difficulties in building a strong team. Christ prepared his team for difficulty: he talked about the possible problems before they arose.[12] In this way the team was encouraged and prepared, so that when the opposition increased, they remembered the promises of their leader to be with them.

Eighth, give your team feed-back. Christ emphasised service and success. 'Well done, good and faithful servant',[13] but he was also ready to point out failure, confusion and error.[14] Leadership is not about being liked — it is about loving and being loved. The leader who loves the team wants only the best for it and will be prepared to overcome the false sense of loyalty which turns a blind eye to the weakness of the team and its individual members.

Ninth, help your team to learn. Christ reviewed the experience of the team as it grew and developed. 'What about you?' he asked them. 'Who do you say I am?'[15] He checked to see that they were taking note of their experience and was always ready to explain his actions and his words.[16]

Tenth, give your team a vision. Christ gave the team something to hope for: a goal, a vision, a dream, a promise. He expected results, expected success, expected progress, and after three years of building his team, when they all seemed to be in disarray, he strengthened them and reminded them of their vision and their calling.[17]

How does your performance in your current team rate alongside the example given in St Matthew's Gospel? Complete the checklist by ticking in the appropriate box.

CHECKLIST FOR TEAM BUILDERS

1 As a person I am clear
   about my work targets

always	A ☐
sometimes	B ☐
rarely	C ☐

2 I lose my temper

never	A ☐
sometimes	B ☐
often	C ☐

3 I find doing what I am told

easy	A ☐
difficult	B ☐
impossible	C ☐

4 I value people for

what they can become	A ☐
what they can do	B ☐
what they have done	C ☐

5 I think confrontation

has its place	A ☐
is wrong for me	B ☐
is always wrong	C ☐

6 My interest in my team members is

extensive	A ☐
superficial	B ☐
very limited	C ☐

7 In my team, problems

are anticipated	A	
take us by surprise	B	
do not exist	C	

8 In my team, members

know exactly how well they are doing	A	
only know when they are doing a good job	B	
never know how they are performing	C	

9 In my team, we review progress

at every meeting	A	
infrequently	B	
never	C	

10 My team is

clear about the future	A	
uncertain about priorities	B	
not interested in the future	C	

To assess your score: for each A, give yourself 10 points; for each B, give yourself 5 points; for each C, give yourself 2 points.

If your total score was over 70, then your potential as a team builder and the potential of your team is high.

If you scored 50 to 70, your performance could be considerably improved. You will find this book of particular help.

If your score was below 50, your team runs a very high risk of failure. It is doubtful whether you will make much progress unless you work through this book with someone else. Who might you choose?

The Need for Change

In this chapter I have been helping you to recognise that there are successful and unsuccessful teams, and that performance is determined by the behaviour of the team members. You have also seen that your own and your team's behaviour falls short of the example that I have chosen in this chapter to illustrate ideal team building. The question now is — what needs to change in your team?

Use the following checklist to identify two changes that would improve the performance of your team:

Checklist for the Team in Which You Wish to See Change

1	Title of the team	
2	Are you the recognised leader?	YES/NO
3	What one change would you like to see take place (a) in the way the team operates?* (b) in the way you operate?*	
4	Does the rest of the team support your desire for change?	YES/NO/DON'T KNOW
5	What three features in the situation would help the team change?	A B C
6	What are the three major obstacles to change?	A B C

* This should be expressed as a target. A target is specific; it can be measured, and it has a time element included. Thus 'To have

a better team' is not a target, but 'To reduce the length of our committee meetings by 30 minutes by end of this year, without reducing the ground covered' would be a target.[18]

What Is a Team?

You may be a member of many teams, and it is likely that membership of some of these teams will overlap, so members of one will be members of another. A team does not exist in a vacuum. Think for a moment about the dictionary definition of a team 'a group of people organised to work together'.[19] Thus a team situation assumes the following:

- a purpose
- a limited life
- a limited membership
- an organisation structure
- an environment.

Let us look at each of these assumptions in turn.

A Purpose

A team needs to have a purpose, a vision, and targets. Purposes are those longer-term statements of intent which describe the *raison d'être* of the team. The purpose may be the constitution, or the mandate, or terms of reference, eg 'to oversee the life and work of the project' or 'to monitor the financial state of the organisation and to recommend to the board appropriate action.' These two statements could be purpose statements for a project management group and a finance committee.

Purpose statements should be written down and shared with each member of the team. Has the team that you have decided to focus on (page 12) a written statement of purpose? If you have no written statement of purpose, then write down now what you believe the purpose to be. When next the team meets, ask all members to write down what they believe the purpose to be. Be ready for surprises!

The purpose of *our* team is:

_____

_____

_____

A Limited Life

A team consists of a number of members, who by nature of their humanity have a limited life. Membership turnover in some teams is high. In most industries and city churches, the turnover in a year is between 20 and 40%, a rate that means that at least 1 member in 5 will change in the course of a year. For some organisations with large student populations, this figure would be much higher, as it would be for teams in cyclical businesses such as hotel and catering, building, and leisure-based industries.

The importance of turnover is simply explained: each time you lose or add a member, you start with a new team! It is also true that a team with high absenteeism or apologies for absence has little chance of successful team building until the matter of regular attendance is dealt with. This is a particular problem for volunteer groups. We often take membership in teams for granted, yet the very fact that an individual does belong can be a powerful influence in developing commitment. Uniforms, badges, rituals, privileges and special knowledge are often used to heighten the sense of membership in teams. What does your team do to make its members feel valued and valuable?

An Organisation Structure

There is a difference between a team and a crowd. A crowd watches a team playing – though in some cases the team outnumbers the crowd! So the difference is not simply size. One of the big differences is organisation. True, a crowd is organised – perhaps according to status, or price of ticket, or age – but it is a temporary organisation. When the crowd has dispersed, the team remains, reviewing its performance, preparing for the next game. There is a degree of permanence to the organisation of the team, and there is an understanding of the relationships between the members – roles, status, responsibilities and authorities are understood, either implicitly or explicitly through written guidelines. Chapter 4 deals in detail with structure. How is your team structured? Can you describe its structure?

Environment

When I talk of environment, I am not referring to the room in which the team meets – although this can be important in terms of the atmosphere in which meetings are conducted – for the immediate physical environment has much less impact than the external environment. All members have come from different parts of this external environment — their homes, their offices, their classes, their departments — and they bring with them the problems, concerns and values of these different environments. It takes time for members to adjust to the new environment of the team. Some members have come from supportive environments; others have come from destructive environments — full of suspicion, intrigue, politics, and competition — with norms and behaviour which need to be laid aside when the team meets. I will deal with meetings in Chapter 8.

Summary
In this chapter we have considered some of the key activities needed for effective team building. We have considered the difference between teams and crowds, and you have committed yourself to some targets (page 27). Before we look further at teams, let me ask what plans you have for achieving your targets. Take time now to write down when and how you are going to act on your targets.

LEADERSHIP and MEMBERSHIP

Chapter 2

The Forgotten Force

There is a strange fascination with leaders and leadership. The shelves are full of books which describe leadership, recount the lives of leaders, and set out ways to become leaders. Books on leadership are probably only outnumbered by books on management. Naturally, since there are more managers in the world than there are leaders, there should be a bigger market for management books! Following that logic, we should be falling over books on the effective worker, the super-subordinate, the one-minute missionary, and the first-class follower! But we are not. Team members are the neglected multitude; followers are the forgotten force, yet without their commitment no leader can sustain a team.

You can probably describe what a team leader needs to be and do, but can you describe what a team member needs to be and do? Let us look at each in turn, first at leadership.

What is Leadership?

What constitutes good leadership? How should a leader behave, and what are the effects of different kinds of leadership? These are some of the questions I will attempt to answer in the first part of this chapter.

We all have our own ideas about how to become leaders. Some believe that leaders are born, not made — you either have it in you or you don't. Astrologers would have us believe that all we are and will be is set for us in our stars. Another approach is to consider the effects of upbringing as the main source of the differences between leaders and followers. Yet others have engaged in studies comparing the physical, intellectual or personality traits of leaders and followers. For example, leaders tend to be taller than their followers. Yet, on the whole, this approach has been disappointing, and there are many examples of leaders who were not bigger; Napoleon, Hitler, Gandhi and many of the leaders of this generation have been smaller than average.

To view the overall situation as the main determining factor in leadership has much to commend it. This view adopts the hypothesis that the behaviour of leaders in one setting may be different from their behaviour in another. This was recognised by bomber crews during World War II. They were allowed to 'mutiny' in emergencies, following a crash behind enemy lines. Although the pilot was in command of the flight in the air, following a crash and any subsequent struggle for survival in enemy territory, the crew could select a different commanding officer whose leadership skills better met the new situation. Although little research has been done in this area, the importance of the situation does suggest the need for flexibility in the practice of selection, training, and use of authority of leaders.

Best Qualified

The situational approach has been extended to focus on the tasks to be done. What this means is that in a given team, one person will lead in one task and someone else in another. One person may be good at gathering information in the group; another may excel at logical analysis of the problem, and so on. So in this approach the group is most effective when responsibility for each of the necessary tasks is taken by the member who is best equipped to handle it. The formal leader of the group will lead only in the instances in which he is best qualified.

The fact that individuals can excel in some aspects of the team's work but not in all has led many writers to adopt a skills approach, claiming that leadership consists of engaging in a number of specific attitudes and behaviours, which can be learned. Another view taken increasingly today, particularly in the religious context, is that leadership is a gift. My own experience of the world is that leadership is an appointment! People end up in leadership positions because they have been put there, and often because no one else would take the job! On the whole, the majority of people in leadership positions are ill-fitted and ill-trained for their responsibilities.

What is your view of leadership? How does your team view leadership? Your answers depend very much on the environment in which your team works. There are no correct answers, only useful answers, in that if the team understands together how it views leadership, then working together will be much easier. This brings me to leadership styles.

Leadership Styles

Leadership style can be thought of as ranging from authoritarian to democratic, to *laissez-faire*. In the authoritarian style, the leader makes the decisions; in the democratic style, the group decides by majority vote; in the *laissez-faire* style, the leader allows each individual to decide for himself, or not to decide at all − if that's how the team feels!

One attempt to integrate these various ideas about leadership was made by Robert Tannenbaum and Warren H Schmidt, and has been described by Peter Wagner.[1] It conceives of leader behaviour ranging along a continuum from the leader-centred approach to the group-centred approach (see overleaf).

Influencing Factors

The choice of leadership style is influenced by a number of forces. The most dominant of these forces is one's own personal value system. If, for example, you value status and position, then you are likely to resent any practices which seem to reduce your authority or power, and you will tend to resist anyone in the team who tries to undermine your position or the position of the leader. I have often seen team leaders trying to encourage participation in decision-making and being blocked by team members who believed that it was the leader's task to make decisions. Our personal values determine to a large extent the style we use and like to work with.

A second factor that influences the choice of leadership style arises from the expectations of the team. I remember working with a team which had only been together for three weeks. The members had come from different organisations and countries

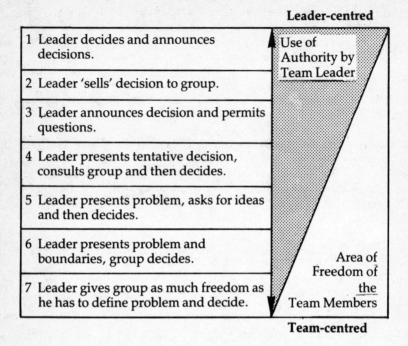

Leadership Styles, *based on the Tannenbaum Schmidt Model* [2]

to provide a new international service. Each had been selected for his or her recognised expertise, and the leader wanted to use a democratic style. What the new team wanted, however, was clear direction – to be told what to do and how to do it! In a new situation, it is often impossible and unwise to try to use highly participative approaches. So the maturity of the team should influence the style that the leader adopts.

In some situations, democratic leadership is not only unwise – it can be very dangerous. In crisis situations – or when time is short – strong, authoritative leadership is required. The good leader is one who can adapt his style to the needs of the team and the situation.

Tendencies

There are of course risks in whatever style you use. If you operate at the leader-centred end of the spectrum, you face the danger of:

– having only one brain in the group – yours!

- focusing only on the task and forgetting the needs of your team
- suppressing creative thinking and running short of ideas
- having to supervise the team constantly to ensure that they do exactly as they have been told
- becoming feared by and isolated from the team members
- running a team of low satisfaction.

Authoritarian styles tend to inhibit the growth of the team members. The team may become highly dependent on the leader and unable to operate without him. But before you start changing your style, what about the dangers of a group-centred approach?

Group-Centred Style

It is important to remember that a group-centred style can often suit the leader − particularly a weak one. This approach helps cover his inconsistency and incompetency, but cover up or not, a group-centred style often is characterised by:

- a leader who is difficult to pin down
- members having to fend for themselves
- a tendency for the group to elect its own leader who, although recognised by the team, will have little or no authority outside the group
- low trust by the group in the 'official' leader
- low morale (see Chapter 9)
- low concern for the task
- a high concern for personal needs and interests
- a fall in the standard of work.

Clearly, a group-centred approach is fraught with difficulties, too, yet it does highlight the need for teams to be concerned for the interests of the members and the relationships within the team.

Somewhere between the two extremes lies a range of acceptable working practices in which a balance is maintained. In addition, the leader of a group that has some permanence will also want to consider some long-term purposes related to the morale, flexibility, and climate of the group. Some long-term purposes are: improved motivation, increased readiness to accept change, improved quality of decisions, better teamwork, and individual development of group members. Most research and experience suggests that team-centred leadership styles are consistent with the pursuit of these long-term purposes.

Balanced Style

A balanced style is not fixed; it is dynamic and responsive to the needs of the leader, the team and the task. Features of such a style are:

- full discussion of problems and involvement of the group
- joint decision making
- work allocation left more to the members themselves once the targets and tasks have been defined
- all brains are used and the climate is supportive of innovation and change
- creative thinking encouraged
- people feel as if they are wanted and there is a strong sense of belonging
- team satisfaction tends to be high and this, in turn, leads to good morale
- work gets done well and effectively.

Leadership Generalisations

From these ideas it is possible to draw some generalisations, since the principles of effective leadership have been known and practised for thousands of years. However, the Ten Commandments have been written down for almost as long; and most people understand them and subscribe to them, too — but most of us find difficulty in keeping them! The same is true of leadership. The principles are straightforward, but the practice requires tremendous self-discipline and frequent self-examination. Here are five conclusions:

1 There is probably no single *right* style of leader behaviour.
2 An effective leader is one who is sensitive to and able to assess the various forces that should influence his behaviour in a given situation.
3 An effective leader is one who can behave comfortably along the whole range of the leadership style continuum, ie he can modify his leadership style to fit the demands of the situation.

4 Generally, there is confusion and frustration when a leader behaves differently from the way the group expects him to behave.
5 An effective leader of a relatively permanent group considers long-range purposes as he chooses his leadership style and operates as near to the group-centred end of the continuum as is possible in any situation.

What is your leadership style? Whatever it is, what you are attempting to do as a leader is basically the same, no matter what your style. You are trying to achieve results — success in the team's chosen field.

Membership

There will always be more followers than leaders, always more players than captains, and it is the quality of membership which in the end will determine the success of the team. It is true that a good leader can inspire a team and cause it to excel, yet without the team's willingness to be led and without their commitment to work together, even the best leader will have short-lived success.

I have worked with leaders in industry who recognised the importance of the team quality. I recall one who had a reputation for trouble shooting. His approach was quite simple: within three months of any appointment, he had identified the weak members of his team and arranged for their replacement by the highest quality he could find. This approach, although somewhat hard, always produced results. Having selected his team, he would then start his team building. Not everyone can or would want to approach his or her team building with this clean-sweep style; most leaders have to work with the material they have inherited or had thrust upon them. This is why membership is so important. I would rather have a mediocre member who knew what membership meant than an outstanding prima donna who left no place on stage for the chorus!

What Does It Take?

What does it take to be an effective member of a team? In its studies of 'superteams', Ashridge Management College found that the good team members' 'actions and attitudes challenge some widely held beliefs.'[3] Good team members exhibit a number of key attitudes:
1 They are active followers.
2 They know when to give and ask for help.

3 They are willing to be led by any of the team members, provided the proposal is seen to be in the best interests of the group.
4 They take their membership seriously and will assume responsibility on behalf of the group in order to avoid disappointments, problems or let-downs.
5 They go out and talk to others.
6 They break bad news before it is too late.
7 They pay great attention to keeping up to date.
8 They set their own standards and work to them.

These are some of the features of the 'super member'. It is quite fascinating to realise that all the characteristics above can be found in the New Testament as the disciples grew under the hand of Jesus, the master team builder.

Functions

John Adair in *Effective Team Building* devotes a whole chapter to the functions of members and describes how each member must contribute to the life of the team in an active way.[4] These contributions may have to do with the task in hand or with the way the team is functioning, particularly in its relationships. Adair describes a number of activities necessary for good teamwork. These activities are the responsibility of each member, not just the leader. There are *task*-oriented activities which are needed to ensure that the team achieves its targets. These task activities include such things as asking questions to make sure that the team has all the information it needs and recording contributions to ensure that the 'group memory' is efficient. In addition, there are *group*-oriented activities which help to keep the team together; these include encouraging others to participate and mediating between opposing parties or ideas. Finally, there are *personal* activities − hobby horses, if you like − which really do not contribute much to the team and have nothing to do with what the team is or needs. In this category are the blocking activities − resisting, disagreeing and opposing because that's what we like to do, or seeking recognition.

Think about your own contributions. Do you tend to be more concerned with:

− what the group is doing?

− how the group is feeling, or

− how you are feeling?

Clearly, there is a wide range of opinions about what it takes to be a good team member. The first requirements that we will examine are motivation and commitment. Unless you are determined to improve your performance as a team member, you will make little progress! Unless you are committed to the well-being of the team, your gains may be at the team's expense, and any skills you acquire may be misused in your own search for excellence.

We can now bring together our two concepts of leadership and membership to help identify the type of team with which you have to deal. The diagram below shows four possible combinations of leadership and membership.

ACTIVE MEMBERSHIP

THE 'DYNAMIC' GROUP	THE 'NOVA' GROUP
THE 'FOLLOWER' GROUP	THE 'ARMCHAIR' GROUP

ACTIVE LEADERSHIP   **PASSIVE LEADERSHIP**

PASSIVE MEMBERSHIP

These four groups are characterised as follows:

The 'Dynamic' Group
- high activity
- high co-ordination
- clear direction
- shared leadership
- co-operation
- commitment to the group

The 'Nova' Group
- high activity
- low co-ordination
- many directions
- confused responsibility
- conflict
- commitment to self

The 'Follower' Group
- reluctant activity
- high control
- clear instruction
- delegation
- hierarchy
- submission
- commitment to leader

The 'Armchair' Group
- low activity
- low control
- no direction
- abdication
- no structure
- apathy
- no commitment

Now check your own group against these features. What is the nature of your group? What would you wish to see changed? How can you begin to make that change?

At first sight, the answers to these questions may be a bit daunting, particularly if you are not the leader, but take courage. In the next chapter we will consider how to develop commitment and motivation. This will help in the process of change that needs to take place in order for your team to develop.

MOTIVATION and COMMITMENT

Chapter 3

Motivation comes from within. You cannot 'motivate' someone; this popular misconception causes much confusion. What is motivation? It consists of the feelings and attitudes we experience when a situation triggers one or more of our basic needs. This emphasis on situation is important since it means that either the leader or the member can create situations in which they or others will be motivated.

My children have been brought up in similar environments, guided by similar parental values, but encouraged to discover their own uniqueness. Each is very different — one is very gregarious, enjoys company, particularly adults, and even as a toddler was always 'getting lost' in stores when he would engage assistants or other customers in conversation. He thrives in company and is never happy with individual pastimes and hobbies, even bird watching and fishing must be with a companion. My younger child, on the other hand, is very self-contained. Monosyllabic responses are the most that adults will prise out of him, unless it is in a competitive setting. He is very much a loner and is never more happy than when he is playing competitive games, racing or 'BMXing' around the garden. Two children, motivated by different situations — one by company, the other by competition. Although time and experience will modify their behaviour, they will continue to respond in different ways to different environments. This is because their basic needs are different. What is meant by 'basic needs':

People and Motivation

Avoiding the jargon of the psychologists, one might say that people have five basic needs:

- to have
- to be
- to do
- to love
- to grow.

This list is based on the work of Abraham Maslow, who did much valuable and pioneering work in the field of human motivation.[1] People's activities are motivated by their desire to satisfy these needs. If leaders wish to provide a team environment in which people are motivated, then they must structure situations so that team members are able to satisfy their needs while also doing what the team requires them to do.

Let us examine each need.

To Have

This need operates at two levels. People want the things necessary to survive, like shelter, food and clothing for themselves and their families — and to a standard which they have defined for themselves as acceptable. Most people have decided upon the level of expenditure that buys the things they want in this category, and up to this level, are highly motivated by money and little else. People are motivated by the chance to earn money — some to a greater and some to a lesser extent, since money will provide for the basic need of having enough to survive.

Once the basic needs are secured, people want to be able to buy what affluent society has persuaded them are 'essentials' — fridges, microwaves and videos; and they may want prestigious possessions — works of art, antiques, large cars and other status symbols.

In the context of the team, 'survival' means continuing membership, plus the status that belonging to the group brings, as well as the sense of security that accompanies the belonging. Thus the leader can create the situation which motivates the 'haves' of this world by providing the member with rewards or a sense of status. Since in most non-commercial teams there is little opportunity for financial reward, the leader must look for other means of satisfying this need. We will look at how this might be done shortly.

To Be

Most people have built for themselves, often subconsciously, a model of the kind of person they wish to be, and to be seen by others to be. It may be to be well known, or to be seen as powerful, with influence over the lives of others. It may be to be respected by particular groups of people, or to be used as a counsellor or an adviser. For some, it might be to be the life and soul of the party, to be the jester among friends and colleagues.

A team member will be highly motivated if achievement of team targets helps him to be the sort of person he wants to be. If the team does not permit him to be what he wants to be, he may have to surround himself with titles, with status symbols, and other things that fool his team mates, and maybe even himself, into believing he is what he wants to be. Alternatively, the member may channel all his energies into other activities outside the team where he receives more encouragement and recognition.

You cannot be a truly effective leader of a team unless you can 'read' the needs of your team members. The team provides an ideal setting for individuals to find satisfaction and acceptance. How can you help team members develop if you do not know what their dreams are? But this is not the responsibility of the leader only; in the effective team, all members are committed to helping their partners develop their sense of value and being.

To Do

We all wish to feel valued and to live meaningful lives. This sense of genuine purpose may come from many sources, like bringing up children, improving working conditions in industry, inventing a new process, making a business tick, and a thousand other things. Your team members will be highly motivated if the team activities contribute to the things they want to do. If not, they will seek their 'doing' satisfaction outside the team. If membership has no meaning; if the tasks are trivial, tedious, not valued or not recognised − then there is little chance of the members putting energy into the team. If you are the leader, you must learn to make each task significant; if you are a member, you should seek to influence the work of the team in such a way that its activities are of value to you.

To Love

Few of us can exist as isolated individuals for long. We need to love and be loved. Each member of your team wants to be wanted. This emotional dimension may seem at first to be only a concern of the family and close friends, but people seek friends within their teams and go to considerable lengths to fit in with the behaviour pattern of their fellow members if it means that they will be accepted. A person is motivated more highly in the team if, while achieving its objectives, he is also satisfying his social needs by winning the affection of those he wishes to count as friends and companions. For some people, the *affiliation motive*, as this need is often called, is very high and dominates all other motives. The strongest, the most independent of us knows that at the bottom of each breath there is an empty place that needs to be filled.

To Grow

Fulfilment comes from growth. My children often talk of 'when I am bigger'. The need to grow is fairly obvious in a small child, and much of it is, of course, to do with stature − the child genuinely wants to physically grow and to overcome the disadvantages of being small. But as the child matures, the growing need shifts into the areas of skill, knowledge and experience, and the cry becomes, 'Let me try!' In most people up to late middle age, the need to grow is fairly strong, unless it has been killed off by negative influences in early life or, more often nowadays, unemployment offering no opportunity to grow at all.

This need to grow should be at its peak in people who have entered adulthood and are wanting to see how far they can stretch themselves. Young people of potential are likely to be motivated by the chance to enlarge their knowledge, skill and experience more than by any of the other motivating factors. Most young folk are seriously under-employed and under-developed, and that is one reason they get bored or angry. If you have young people in your team, keep them busy; use their energy and enthusiasm. It is likely that most of the apostles were under 30 years of age and some were in their teens when

Jesus called them. So do not under-estimate the potential of the young. (By the way, what is the average age of your team?)

But growth is not the prerogative of the young. Whatever the age of your team, each member has an infinite capacity to learn. Consider what motivates the members of your team. Do you know how to create the environment which will cause them to give their best?

Positive and Negative Motivation

Certain team features such as working conditions, holidays and financial reward may be 'negative' factors in motivation. Short-comings in these areas cause dissatisfaction in the team members and generate an unwillingness to contribute fully, but changes for the better are soon taken for granted and probably do not provide any greater satisfaction. Therefore, though the removal of these irritations cannot be used to provide a motivating climate, their presence will certainly discourage the team.

On the other hand, features such as challenge, opportunities to use skill and experience, responsibility, opportunity to be and do and grow are positive factors in motivation. Their presence will get the best results out of the team members; their absence will give rise to mediocre performance, absenteeism or high turnover.

Note that you cannot trade negative factors for positive ones. They are independent. For example, no fringe benefits will compensate for lack of opportunity, and no amount of challenge will compensate for the irritation caused by members being refused entry into the directors' dining room!

Performance and Reward

The team leader is responsible for creating an environment in which the team members are motivated to perform effectively. Obviously, the greater the opportunity to have needs satisfied, the greater the motivation. The diagram overleaf illustrates the situation needed for effective motivation. It shows that motivation is influenced by four major factors.

Individuals' Current Needs

We have seen how individuals' basic needs influence the degree of motivation experienced. From the example of my sons, we noted that we all adopt basic patterns of behaviour to satisfy our needs. These patterns are dynamic and will change from situation to situation and from time to time. Thus in the

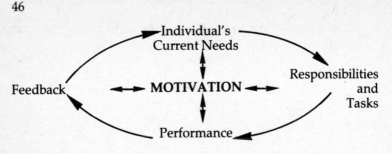

A Model for Motivation

team situation, the leader must be aware of the current needs of the individual. If you have new members in your team, one of their current needs will be to gain acceptance within the team; this will be less of a need for someone who has been a long-serving member and whose past contribution is highly valued. But whether we are old or new members, accepted or still to prove ourselves, the tasks we are given in the team are important to us.

Responsibilities and Tasks

We all respond with enthusiasm to certain tasks. Gardening is fun, but weeding is a chore! Preparing a dinner is an opportunity for creativity and skill; washing up is somewhat less exciting! Doing the job is challenging; but completing the paperwork is tedious, and so on. I never fail to be amazed at the variety of jobs which excite and occupy people for whole careers. A team is a microcosm of this universal phenomenon. Once again, there is the challenge to the leader to fit the tasks and responsibilities to the individual member so that, as far as possible, each obtains job satisfaction.

I was asked to do a team-building week for an American company operating in Europe. As part of the preparation, I visited the headquarters and sat in on the management team to observe its operations. It was like many meetings – long, tedious and uninspiring, and followed by even longer, more tedious and even less inspiring minutes! I needed no further explanation as to why a team-building activity had been requested. I followed up this first meeting with individual interviews and then visits to each of the departmental team meetings. These gatherings were very different; in them the managers were animated, purposeful and direct in contrast with their earlier performance. Why this difference? It was because in their own meetings they had organised things in such a way that their tasks and responsibilities suited their gifts, skills and styles of management. A month later, I took the team away for three days and helped them restructure the group in such a way that each member was able to contribute on the basis of those tasks which provided him with motivation. Suddenly the team was filled with ideas about how to develop the business. The meetings became animated, crisp, and a pleasure to attend.

It is true, of course, that there are some tasks which are never going to inspire and for these we may need Mary Poppins' spoonful of sugar, or a good example − the leader washing his followers' feet. But too often the leader keeps all the interesting tasks to himself; he sets the agenda, chairs the meeting, takes the minutes, writes them up and denies the team and the individuals the opportunity to develop and grow. Such leadership is self-centred, arrogant and patronising and is unlikely to provide the environment in which members can be motivated.

The team leader must provide more than the environment in which members will be motivated; he must also provide the opportunity for the team to perform. There are two key ingredients needed for effective performance: targets and opportunity. The leader should agree with each member the tasks to be done and the results to be achieved; in other words, the leader should provide targets and should then stand back to give the member an opportunity to perform. By providing targets and opportunity, the leader will help create a climate in which the members' motivation will be aroused. Let us examine these in turn.

Targets In practice, it has been found that team members are often unclear about the results they are expected to achieve. They do not know what is required. These 'grey areas' are a potential cause of insecurity and over-caution. If a member's first thought is 'Is it my responsibility to get this done?' then a state of uncertainty develops which often impedes initiative. In my seminar work, delegates quote 'unclear targets' as one of the greatest sources of stress on the job. It is therefore essential that a member should be able to agree with his team leader the −

1 overall purpose of the member's role − why am I here?
2 results to be achieved to fulfil this role − what have I to do?
3 performance standards and control methods which relate to these results − how thorough, detailed and extensive a job is needed?
4 limitations of authority of the role − how far can I go? How much can I spend?
5 short-term priorities which must be satisfied to integrate the member's role with the group's targets and priorities − what

should I do first? Who needs to know? Who can help? By when?

A discussion based on the above is particularly useful when set alongside a list of 'duties and responsibilities' (see page 53).

This may sound a formal approach, but it can be done in a simple briefing when a new member joins the team, and certainly items 2-5 should be made explicit each time some action is agreed. There is some debate about whether the leader should decide these details or discuss and agree them with the member. This will depend on the leader's style (page 34) and on the individual's needs.

An opportunity to perform Even if careful thought has been given to everyone's role in the team, a badly conceived control structure could mean that hard-working and able members are not able to contribute effectively to the overall targets and priorities.

Some useful questions to ask if effort is to be clearly directed and controlled are:

- is there an effective division of the work in the team?
- are responsibilities and targets clearly understood?
- is there a sound line of command?
- is there provision for control and accountability?

How many times have you heard someone say, 'Oh, I thought *you* were doing that', or 'I didn't realise that was *my* job'? These problems arise because insufficient attention has been paid to the division and allocation of the work. Before each meeting of the team comes to an end, run through what has been agreed and who is expected to do what by when. To give someone the opportunity to perform means giving them the space, time, trust and the resources needed. The leader who is constantly checking up on the progress of work only serves to delay it. Set a time for the task and, if necessary, a time to review progress; then let the team get on.

One vital area, particularly in new teams or when you have a new member, is that of the interface between responsibilities. Many a friendship has been ruined by a poor team leader who has created confusion between the responsibilities of members. So the leader must ensure that the roles and responsibilities of individual members do not clash and that all the tasks are covered.

Feed-back

This is the fourth element in our model for motivation. Members like to know how they are getting on. Unless the leader can measure to what extent the team is succeeding and where special attention should be focused to overcome obstacles, it is impossible for the team to perform well. Thus it is essential that the leader should get adequate information to enable him to take supportive action in the key areas of the team's work.

The form and frequency of information is important. Too much information can paralyse action; too little can create dangerous ignorance. Systematic, regular feed-back is required, to:

- check results against targets
- encourage better setting of targets
- make better decisions
- give guidance and
- take corrective action.

Besides adequate day-to-day information in order to carry out his leadership, it is the responsibility of every leader to assess the performance of his team members. Done properly, this strengthens the quality of relationship between leader and team. (We will come to this in detail in Chapter 11.) The feed-back not only provides guidance and encouragement, but also helps to identify training and development needs.

Something like 80% of a team member's development — knowledge, skills and attitudes — will occur in the team setting. Systematic guidance by the leader, and the right kind of environment, are both necessary for learning. Opportunities should be sought to broaden skills, to teach new techniques and enable the team to operate with members from other teams. These activities can take place in the day-by-day working of the team. There are now some good text-books to help team members develop, in particular *The Unblocked Manager*.[2] (In Chapter 13, I deal with training and coaching in some detail.)

Feed-back is a form of reward, and this is important when the rewards often have to be subjective. The rewards a leader can give for performance come in three levels:

1 the obvious rewards, clearly understood by all:
   eg greater responsibility — given or accrued; more interesting tasks; greater freedom, etc

2   the more subtle rewards which satisfy the less obvious, or
     undisclosed needs that the team member has, which may
     probably only be recognised by the member and the leader:
     eg opportunity to express talent or skill; chance to develop
     new capabilities; chance to derive and exercise power
3   the rewards that address the private needs the team member
     is trying to satisfy, which he may (or may not) be aware of in
     himself and would be unlikely to reveal to the leader − even
     if he suspects the leader may have recognised them:
     eg recognition for effort, if not success; an opportunity to
     influence; encouragement of acceptance by certain members
     of the group.

In the commercial or industrial setting, the team member's
need to be rewarded according to his contribution means that
the company must have a progressive salary policy, bonus
structure and plan for promotion. A reward structure should:

− reward members equitably in relation to each other, and their
personal contribution to the team

− provide an incentive to better performance, rather than
merely reward past services

− have a sensible relationship to rewards in the same job, or
geographical location, which are offered by other companies

− be flexible in operation, not mechanistic and bureaucratic.

Promotion is another way of rewarding a team member's
performance. However, in the voluntary sector, such rewards
are often not open to the leader. Nevertheless, good
performance must be rewarded since this is a means of
encouragement. Here are some examples taken from the first
century AD as Jesus dealt out encouragement to his followers:

− recognise performance: 'Well done, good and faithful
servant.'[3] Too often, leaders are reluctant to give positive feed-
back.

− recognise publicly: 'Blessed are you, Simon son of Jonah.'[4]

− give, or offer more responsibility: 'Feed my lambs.'[5]

− give, or offer more visible, 'prestigious' tasks: 'Take care of
my sheep.'[6]

− provide for more opportunity to have needs met: 'Mary has
chosen what is better, and it will not be taken away from her.'[7]

Highly Motivated

We have seen that team members will be highly motivated when –

1 they understand and approve of the targets towards which they are working.
2 they have helped to set the targets and planned their own method of working.
3 they have control over information, which permits them to measure their own performance.
4 the targets are challenging and help them to develop.
5 checks and controls are the minimum necessary, but effective.
6 people co-operate with each other, through mutual understanding of their responsibilities and priorities.
7 emphasis is on using strengths, not correcting weaknesses.
8 achievement is rewarded.

But how can we ensure that the motivation is correctly directed? One answer to this is to have written statements of expected performance in the team – a job description that helps team members understand what is expected.

Job Descriptions

Conflict in the team will lessen if there are clear targets, good planning, and the wise recognition and use of skills. Tension will ease with careful delegation and good communication. But the tool that is perhaps most valuable in helping relationships within the team is the job description. This helps to answer the four questions any team member is likely to ask from time to time:

1 What is my job? This deals with targets and priorities.
2 Am I doing it all right? This deals with supervision, training and evaluation.
3 Where do I go for help? This deals with the resources, skills and support of other team members.
4 What am I supposed to be doing? How do I relate to others in the work group?

In attempting to address these questions the job description will:

– clarify relationships between team members' responsibilities, thus avoiding overlaps, gaps and misunderstandings.
– help define the team structure.

- provide the first step in actual job measurement and evaluation (see Chaper 12).
- help introduce new people to the team; it can thus be valuable in the orientation process for new members.
- help identify training needs.

A job description should be a simple, single-page document. It should be kept up to date, reviewed at least annually; and, of course, it should be available for all members of the team to see. The following pages give an outline and an example of a typical job description. See also page 133 where a job description is given for the chairman of a board.

Summary
Commitment comes from motivation, which in turn, comes from an amalgam of our personal needs, from the situation and from the demands placed upon us. Although you cannot motivate others, it is possible for you to create an environment in which team members will be truly self-motivated and give of their best to the work of the team. Think about each member of your team. What situations and tasks motivate them? Complete the table at the end of this chapter.

TEAM JOB DESCRIPTION FORMAT

Job Title

Prepare a job title, specifically and carefully worded which describes the role of the team member.

Basic Objective

Summarise the job objective, including the scope, the nature of the responsibilities and the reporting relationships. It should capture the essence of the job. What does it exist to do?

Duties and Responsibilities

Describe the specific responsibilities, emphasising the most important ones. State the nature of contacts within and outside of the team. Indicate the type of responsibility when relating to other team members.

Qualifications

Indicate the level and the type of skills needed.
Describe the experience required, for example, the type and the number of years.
Specify special or technical skills required, listing the licences or qualifications necessary.
State any language capabilities required and desired.
Try to differentiate between qualifications *necessary* and *desirable*.

Conditions

Describe the amount of time to be committed to the team.

Date

Date the job descriptions; have it signed by the team leader and the team member.

Job Holder _____

Team Leader _____

JOB DESCRIPTION FOR THE PAROCHIAL COUNCIL COMMITTEE SECRETARY

Job Title: PCC Secretary

Basic Objective:
To ensure that the PCC, Parochial Church Meetings and Vestry Meetings are thoroughly planned and efficiently operated.

Duties and Responsibilities
1   To assist the Vice-Chairman to organise the Vestry and Parochial Church Meetings and meetings of the PCC, by ensuring that information and documents about them are circulated by the required times.
2   To keep records of meetings and, in particular, records of decisions of the PCC, in order to remind those concerned of agreed procedures and to draw attention during discussion to relevant decisions.
3   To ensure that decisions of the PCC or the Parochial Church Meeting are known and understood by those responsible for implementing them.
4   To attend meetings of the Standing Committee.
5   To conduct the correspondence of the PCC but not of its committees or groups (other than the Standing Committe).
6   To keep the Secretary of the Diocesan and Deanery Synods informed of his address and telephone number.
7   To ensure that meeting places are properly prepared.
8   To undertake such other duties as the PCC may reasonably request.

Appointed by and responsible to:
The PCC

Qualifications
A church member for at least five years; a member of the PCC; able to drive; able to type.

Conditions
Must be willing to allocate an average of three hours per week to the job.

ASSESSMENT OF TEAM MEMBERS' MOTIVATION

Name of Team Member	What Motivates This Member?
1 Me	*Situations* *Tasks*
2	*Situations* *Tasks*
3	*Situations* *Tasks*
4	*Situations* *Tasks*
5	*Situations* *Tasks*
6	*Situations* *Tasks*
7	*Situations* *Tasks*

PART 2
Acquiring the Skills

TEAM STRUCTURE

CHAPTER 4

We come now to one of the most neglected areas of teamwork. We have considered how to build commitment and also how to establish a foundation of skills, but skilled people with high motivation are only the building blocks for our team — they are not the end product. The team does not exist for the member, rather each member exists for the team.

In this chapter we shall consider the various ways in which teams can be structured — or organised — in order to make the best use of the members' skills and motivation.

What is Structure?

Teams are held together by the relationships which exist between the members. These relationships may be formal, so that in some teams the structure is made clear by — for example — where you sit, or the number on your back, or the pips on your shoulder. Alternatively, the relationships may be informal, as might be the case in many social groups — the only structure being whose round it is! Yet even in these informal settings, the skills are still recognised — 'Give us a song, Dave' or 'Tell that one about the bishop, Mary.'

The importance of structure is fivefold; it:

- establishes roles for each member
- sets down patterns for communication
- gives authority
- allows for delegation of responsibility
- provides guidelines for relationships.

Without a recognised structure, the team will have considerable difficulty in functioning.

Team Roles

We know that most teams have a chairperson, a secretary and a treasurer. Larger groups may have vice-chairs or deputies, but for many of us, this is the extent of our role distribution and the roles dictate the structure. Clearly, in very large groups this could prove a problem — too many Indians and not enough chiefs! — and this problem would not be solved by creating a large number of roles. John Adair describes 27 possible roles in his book *Effective Team Building*, all of which are linked to the task, team and individual activities.[1] The difficulties of the inter-relationships with so many roles are considerable. Thus role and structure must be considered together.

Communication and Structure

In Chapter 5 we will consider the skills needed for effective one-to-one communication. In the team setting, the practice will vary with the structure. How does communication operate in your team? Does the chairperson tell everyone at once, or is information passed out to the secretary, then to the members? Do people communicate 'through the chair' at team meetings, or is direct interaction between members possible? Is most of the business conducted in the team meeting, or in pre-meetings, or corridors or loos? How frequently do or should the members communicate? The answers to all these questions will be heavily influenced by the structure.

Ashridge Management College made a study of teams. The researchers noticed the importance of communication when the team was apart and emphasised the need to 'Have a good secretary, co-ordinator or personal assistant for the leader, who can act as an information puller and pusher. This person should always be asking, "who needs to know what and when?"[2] An important aspect of groups is shown here: the relationships that exist in the outside world are often carried into the team.

Authority

Who is the leader, and how does the leader relate to others? In Chapter 3 we saw how important the *style* was in determining the relationship between the leader and followers; now we must add *structure*. Often the structure of the team will be determined for the leader, and the duties, responsibilities and limits of authority will be spelt out in the team constitution, job description or some other document. In these cases, the leader must work within the constraints of structure, for any change to the constitution may take years rather than weeks to implement, particularly if the constitution has some legal standing. Thus the authority of the leader and the team can be severely restricted or enhanced by the structures applied.

Where greater flexibility exists in team size and structure, then this should be used to provide the relationships which best suit the team's current membership and tasks. (This is most obvious in football, where the structure of the team is altered according to the opposing team's style of play.)

When was the last time your team was restructured? Are you constrained by traditional structures? Are you trying to use today's techniques with yesterday's concepts of organisation?

Delegation

Whether and how much delegation of authority and responsibility takes place is often dictated by the style of leadership; however, the structure will also contribute to the ease with which this sharing out of tasks is done. It is much easier to delegate in small teams since the communication and follow-up are easy. In large teams the problems of keeping track of progress discourage delegation, unless there is a structure which allows the follow-up to be delegated. Rules for delegation are:

1 Provide complete information on the task. What is the target? When is it to be completed? What standards are you expecting?
2 Define precisely the limits of responsibility of the person in relation to the task. Satisfy yourself that he understands them, eg How much money can be spent, what equipment can be used, to whom can he talk?

62

3 Don't provide the answers, but help the person to find them. Where might he look for information, guidance, etc?
4 Don't make the decisions for the person — give him as much freedom as you can.
5 Do not be hasty in criticising mistakes. You might not have made the same mistake, but you might have made another.
6 Follow up on delegation. Agree when you will check to see that progress is being made.
7 Encourage the initiative of the other person so that he can cope with emergencies if they arise, rather than running back to you.
8 Never publicly countermand a decision taken by the person to whom you have delegated. Allow him to reverse it.
9 Back up your people to the limit that your conscience will allow.
10 Accept responsibility for all decisions that you delegate.[3]

Relationships

In a team of 5 people, 20 one-to-one relationships are possible. A team of 12 increases this number to 132, and this does not take into account the fact that sub-groups can form within the larger team — making the number of possible combinations of relationship into the 1000s! In larger teams, structures help to clarify and simplify the 'who does what?' question.

Possible Structures

There are four basic structures upon which all team and organisation shapes are based. These are:

— the line structure

— the staff structure

— the functional structure and

— the matrix structure.

They vary according to their different emphases — whether on the leader, the task or the team.

In the following diagrams, I will use a code to show authority. This will help us understand the significance of some of the team structures.

 indicates direction of communication

● means a position of full authority

◓ means a position of delegated authority

○ means no authority

The Line Structure: Focus on Leadership

The *line structure* places its emphasis on authority.

The line structure emphasises authority

A says to B, 'Do it, and do it now.' The structure is hierarchical; A is superior to B, and B is subordinate to A. Thus the chairperson says to the member, 'This is the way I want it done.'

  Structures can actually be chosen to focus the relationships on different aspects of the team. For example, a Prime Minister may structure the cabinet to focus either on the leader or on the team of ministers as a whole. The choice is the leader's. Where there is a strong leader − energetic, charismatic, visionary − the structure adopted is often designed to ensure that the leader makes all major decisions and controls all the activities. This is called the *entrepreneurial structure* and is the simplest form of a line structure: when the leader says, 'Jump!' everyone jumps! Using our code, the structure looks like this:

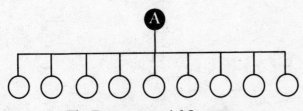

The Entrepreneurial Structure

In the team setting, the entrepreneurial leader is the chairperson, convener, president, etc. Some of the advantages and disadvantages of this type of structure are set out in the table below:

THE ENTREPRENEURIAL STRUCTURE	
Advantages	**Disadvantages**
1 Strong Control	1 Depends on One Brain
2 Fast Response	2 Under-utilisation of Team
3 Very Flexible	3 Limited Development of Team Members
4 Clear Direction	4 Often Short of Information
5 Easy Communication	5 Problems of Conflict with Other Teams

A variation on the entrepreneurial structure is the *cabinet structure* in which − with the focus still very much on the leader − an inner circle of advisers or deputies is formed. This is useful in larger groups of 10 or more members. It was used by Jesus and his apostles. He had an inner circle of friends − Peter, James and John − who were privy to special information and experiences.[4] It is a difficult structure to operate since it runs the risk of a 'we/they' split. We can represent the cabinet structure this way:

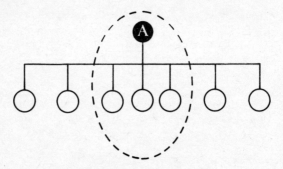

A Cabinet Structure

The three members of the inner cabinet have no additional authority, only that which comes from having more information. Here are some of the advantages and disadvantages of the cabinet structure:

THE CABINET STRUCTURE	
Advantages	**Disadvantages**
1 All the Advantages of the Entrepreneurial Structure Plus –	1 Over-dependency on Leader
2 Shared Vision	2 Risk of Team Split
3 Better Information Flow	3 Low Use of Total Resources
4 Improved Decision Taking	4 Poor Development of Some Members
5 Greater Commitment	5 Risk of a Conflict of Loyalty

The Staff Structure: Focus on Support

The *staff structure* emphasises support. Its main interest is to ensure that the activities of the team are facilitated and the team leader's targets achieved.

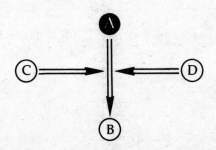

The staff structure emphasises support

The staff organisation asks, 'How can I help?' B is responsible to A, while C and D provide support. In organisational terms, C and D may be the personnel department or the administration services. In the team setting, the support is often supplied by the vice-chairperson and the secretary, both of whom may advise the chairperson A on the tasks given to B – a team member.

Still with some emphasis on the leadership, the staff structure is in fact a development of the cabinet structure. In the staff structure, the inner circle is formally recognised as a permanent support not only to the leader, but also to the whole team. A good example of this would be in the case of a climbing expedition in which the translator and the guide, although reporting to the expedition leader, would be available to give help to any of the expedition team. Note that the staff members have no authority.

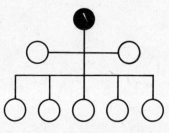

A Typical Staff Structure

In teams, the staff positions are usually filled by secretaries and deputies.

THE STAFF STRUCTURE	
Advantages	**Disadvantages**
1 Strengthens the Leadership	1 Risk of Leader Creating Inner Cabinet
2 More Support Available to the Leader and Team	2 Leader Spends Less Time with Team and More with Staff
3 Leader Can Off-load Tasks to Staff Members	3 Often Conflict of Roles Between Staff and Team
4 Team Has Additional Sources of Information	4 Staff Members Begin to Generate Work for Leader and Team
5 Leader Can Concentrate on Priorities	5 Risk of Takeover Bid by Senior Staff Member

The Functional Structure: Focus on Tasks

So far I have emphasised structures that place their focus on the leader. There are, in addition, a number of structures that have quite a different emphasis: that is, on the talents and gifts of the team as a whole. The first of these is the *functional structure*, which emphasises role. Each member has a function, a specific area of interest and responsibility. For example, A might be in charge of finance, B of marketing, and C of production.

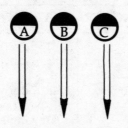

The functional structure emphasises role

A is not responsible to B or C but all would report upward, eventually, to one boss. A has no authority over B, nor B over A. A is charged with one set of tasks, B with a quite different set of tasks. A may be required to provide information to B and C, while B might provide A and C with statistics.

The functional structure also encapsulates the idea of delegated authority − for the first time, we are introducing a hierarchical system. This is shown in our code as follows:

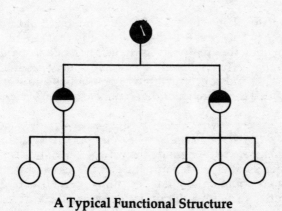

A Typical Functional Structure

68

Such a structure could fit, for example, in a church, where one 'function' could relate to children's work and the other to work with the elderly, or it could represent a geographic split — north and south. The number of functions is not limited, other than by the fact that it becomes increasingly difficult for the leader to keep in touch. The functional heads will have a degree of authority — agreed by the leader — to enable decision making in their teams.

THE FUNCTIONAL STRUCTURE	
Advantages	**Disadvantages**
1 Good Use of Resources	1 Introduces Major Interactions Between the Functions
2 Helps in the Development of Members	2 Risk of Competition for Resources
3 Clear Areas of Responsibility	3 We/They Split Possible
4 Good Control	4 Slower Communication
5 Improved Focus on the Task	5 Risk of Leader Becoming Isolated

The functional structure is the most common in industry and commerce, but its greatest disadvantage is that it emphasises difference. For this reason, it is sometimes called the *differentiated structure*. This high-lighting of the differences has led to much conflict and concern within organisations and teams and has prompted the search for other types of structure.

The Matrix Structure: Focus on the Team
All structures create boundaries between people, sections — or in larger settings — departments, functions, and even locations. Where there are boundaries, things can go wrong: communications break down, priorities differ, conflicts arise, etc. In

order to try to overcome some of these problems, the *matrix structure* may be used. Basically, the matrix gives authority and responsibility to people in more than one area. Thus A is responsible for B and C. It also means that D has two bosses!

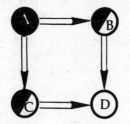

The matrix structure emphasises team interaction

It is a more complex structure, but it does help integrate the teams involved. It also reduces the disadvantages of the functional arrangement. We may encounter structures that emphasise team interaction in two forms: the *multi-disciplinary team structure*, which is in effect a mini-matrix, and the total-matrix structure.

The multi-disciplinary structure recognises the skills of each member and looks to each member for leadership at the appropriate time. Thus although there may be a team leader, the leader's role is mainly one of organising rather than leading. The structure therefore is flexible, and all members have authority in their own fields. We can represent this as shown:

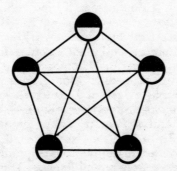

A Multi-disciplinary Team Structure

The 'leader' is often called the 'co-ordinator' or the 'facilitator' to signify the shared authority pattern.

THE MULTI-DISCIPLINARY STRUCTURE	
Advantages	**Disadvantages**
1 Maximum Use of Skills	1 Needs Strong Self-discipline
2 Helps in the Development of Members	2 Team Is Vulnerable to 'Hijacking' by a Strong Member
3 Very Flexible	3 Takes Time to Get up to Speed
4 Develops Strong Team Loyalty	4 Decision Making Can Be Lengthy
5 High Quality Decisionmaking	5 Balance is Easily Disturbed by Membership Change

One limitation of this structure is size. It is not often practical to have more than seven members. Above this number, relationship problems become a major distraction. It is just this problem which the total matrix structure seeks to address.

A matrix structure is like a net or fabric with the warp and weft threads providing direction and control. Let us consider an example before we look at the structural diagram. Imagine a team of sales people doing door to door selling of perfume, cosmetics, watches, jewellery and lingerie – all light-weight products with reasonably high price tags. The team consists of 25 sales representatives and they cover a town of 250,000 people. Each rep has some 3,000 homes to call on, and the town is divided into five areas – north, south, east, west and central each with a supervisor. See the structure opposite. In this structure the five area supervisors B to F all report to A, the regional director. B to F, in turn, have reporting to them five representatives, B1 to B5, etc. Now it could be structured entirely differently, set up on the basis of products – perfume, cosmetics, watches, jewellery and lingerie. This would be very useful if the pattern of sales was different from area to area, eg lingerie in the centre of town, cosmetics in the west, etc. What the matrix does is attempt to give you the best of both worlds. Each supervisor will be given responsibility for both a local area

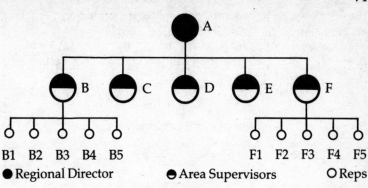

Regional Director   •Area Supervisors   OReps

The Basis of the Matrix

and a product range across the whole city. The structure would look something like this:

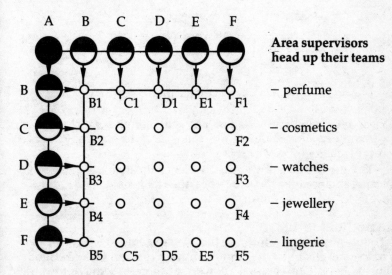

Same area supervisors head up the products across all areas

The Matrix Organisation

The area supervisors B to F still report to the regional director A, but now, in addition to their area responsibilities for their five representatives (shown on the vertical axis), each is given responsibility across the whole city for one product. Each representative now has two bosses and each area team has its own specialist in the five product ranges covered.

For areas and products, you can read functions, age groups, sexes, activities, etc. So, for example, in a church setting you could have a matrix made up of:

- youth work
- senior citizens' activities
- women's work
- men's work
- children's work

as the 'areas' of the church's activities. The other axis of the matrix could be made up from the functions common to all activities, such as:

- worship
- stewardship
- outreach
- mission
- pastoral care.

Each member of the leadership, whether the parish council committee, the elders, or the presbytery, would have responsibility for two areas.

The great value of the matrix lies in its ability to keep large teams and organisations together. (See table opposite.)

Another Option

Trends at work now indicate that we are going to see greater use of the *core group structure* in the future. Professor Charles Handy in his book *Organisations* shows that there is a move towards wider use of contractors.[5] This will increase because of the high cost of full-time labour, the rapid shifts in business activities, the higher levels of unemployment and the fact that fewer people are prepared to commit themselves for life to one organisation.

In the team setting, this would mean the establishment of a small permanent core who would be supplemented by the use of 'seconded' or 'co-opted' members − people who would join the team for specific tasks or times, and then withdraw when the need for their skills was over. This structure can be represented as shown opposite.

THE MATRIX STRUCTURE	
Advantages	**Disadvantages**
1 Good Control	1 Requires Extra Management Effort
2 People Are Informed	2 Uses More Time for Generating Information
3 Good Variety in the Work	3 Requires More Knowledge to Do the Job, Therefore Extra Training Time Needed
4 Holds the Team Together	4 Very Slow to Change
5 Once Established, It Is Not Easily Disturbed	5 Depends on a Good Supply of Skilled Leaders

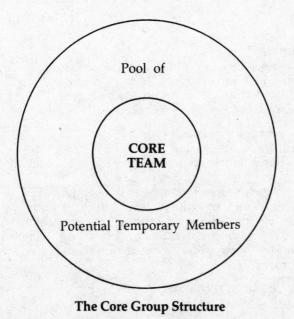

The Core Group Structure

The advantages and disadvantages are shown below.

THE CORE GROUP STRUCTURE	
Advantages	**Disadvantages**
1 Flexible Use of Resources	1 No Sense of 'Belonging' for the Contractors
2 Very Responsive to Work Demands	2 Risk of Being Overwhelmed by 'Outsiders'
3 Cheap to Run	3 Small Is Vulnerable
4 All the Advantages of a Small Group	4 Core Group Can Become Simply Administration with a Loss of Job Satisfaction
5 Can Involve Large Numbers of People Over a Period of Time	5 Group Always Has a Sense of Being in Transition

Summary

Your team will work well when the structure it adopts is appropriate to its environment, its membership skills, its leadership style and vision. There is no one best structure for a team, but certain guide-lines can be followed:

1 Keep your team as small as possible.
2 With 10 members or more, create an inner cabinet.
3 Delegate as much responsibility as possible and for large groups make use of sub-committees.
4 Use a structure which addresses the key problems for your team, eg control, co-ordination or conflict resolution.
5 Be flexible and review your structure regularly − but not frequently. It probably takes 6 to 12 months for a new structure to settle down. Ideally, a structure should be given three years to mature.

How is your team structured?

TEAM SKILLS

Chapter 5

A major reason for people leaving teams is their inability to 'get along'. They seem to be unable to mesh their needs and aspirations and their way of doing things with those of the people with whom they work. Surprisingly, people who may get along poorly in one team often do well together in a different one. It all seems to be a question of fit.

There are a number of phrases in our language which use the term 'fit': 'If the cap fits, wear it' and 'If your face fits, you will succeed', etc. These are alluding to suitability – does the situation or the description fit (or suit) you? In the world of sport, there are many examples of *fit*. A player is put on the transfer list because his performance is low and he is not a saleable commodity; another team signs him on only to discover that they have a world class player on their hands, who fits perfectly into their team.

Misfits also abound, those players who seem to cause trouble wherever they go, despite their very obvious skills. So 'fit' has more to it than skill, for a skilled team member may not fit one particular situation. When we use the term 'face fit', we bring in a new dimension to the issue of suitability. Now it has nothing to do with skill but to do with acceptability — are you one of us? The 'us' can be defined by education, race, political persuasion, religious belief, accent, where you live, or even what or how you eat!

Culture, Groups, and the 'Fit'

When a group has been together for some time, it establishes a set of rules, often unwritten, that forms the basis of their relationships. These rules become the norms for the group — the acceptable normal behaviour. All members abide by these norms; new members must quickly learn the norms if they are to fit in. Failure to abide by the norms will soon lead to sanctions by the team. Continuing breach of the codes of behaviour will result in expulsion. In his book *Gods of Management*[1] Charles Handy describes different types of culture which are commonly found in organisations. These range from very rigid cultures where there are many rules and regulations (bureaucracies), to very flexible cultures where almost anything goes and almost anyone will fit, provided progress is made. As we consider skills, it is important to remember that there is more, much more to success in teams than simply learning what to do and what is your part in the tasks of the group.

What Is It That Fits?

Every team wants people who 'fit in.' A plethora of psychological and physiological tests, and our own experience, have demonstrated that different individuals seem to be particularly equipped to carry out certain kinds of tasks, to play certain roles, to respond to certain situations in a team. Business organisations realise this and attempt to describe the qualifications required for a position in such a way as to attract those talents and experiences most likely to meet the requirements of the position, as well as to sift out those less likely to fit. Finding the 'right person for the right job' is an important skill for any team leader. Without this skill, the turnover of members in the team will be high.

That Synergistic Combination

Most of us have had the experience of seeing how the addition or subtraction of one person from a group can have a major impact on the group's performance. Something very special happens when 'the right combination' of people come together as a working team. It is not always a question of the right leader. Often, the addition of one person who has a particular skill makes all the difference. Perhaps it is the visionary on whose ideas others can build. It may be a person with that wonderful gift of being able to pour oil on troubled waters. At other times, it is someone who can take the ideas of others and restate them in ways which make them both interesting and understandable to the whole team.

The potential power of the team is that it can bring together the skills of different individuals in a synergistic combination so that the whole is greater than the sum of the parts. St Paul recognised this in the first century AD. For him, the good team was like a body in which all the parts functioned appropriately: 'If the whole body were an eye, where would the sense of hearing be? If the whole body were an ear, where would the sense of smell be? But, in fact, God has arranged the parts in the body, every one of them, just as he wanted them to be. If they were all one part, where would the body be?'[2] We can see how ridiculous it is to regard one person, eg the chairperson, as being all that is needed to run the team.

Finding a Better Fit

How might we go about finding a better fit between individual skills and the needs of the team? The following four suggestions will help. First, we need to state the technical skills needed for the job, as well as the kind of experience required of the person.

Second, we need to go further than thinking about the position in the team as a cog or a gear in a machine. People not only function, they also relate. So we need to consider what relationship skills will be needed in the particular group in which this person will work.

Third, we need to devise interview questions that help us to determine how a person has exercised his or her skills in the past. Here the assumption is that if a person is skilled, he will have shown the skill by using it. To do this we shall need to know what skills we are searching for.

Fourth, we need to tell new team members the results of our exploration into their skills. Many people may not have recognised that they are skilled. Part of the training and developing of your team members should be to help them discover those things they do well. One way to help this discovery process is to ask each team member to write about the situations in which they have felt particularly effective or successful.

Team Skills

What skills are needed for effective teamwork? Many approaches have been developed in recent years, and all seem to have contributed in some way to the general understanding of how groups function and what is needed for effective performance. John Adair's work focuses on the leader and leadership behaviour.[3] The work of the Ashridge Management College has majored on the environment and the activities of the team.[4] Mike Woodcock[5] believes that success is dependent on the way people play together, while Geoffrey Mills relates success to a sense of responsibility.[6] Rather than create a new approach, I will attempt to synthesise the elements from past and current writers that I have found to work effectively time and time again.

But a word of caution before we begin this section: every team is unique. You cannot force-fit skills or attitudes into a team and expect it to perform. An effective team is more a work of art than a plastic mould. Use this chapter first to understand yourself and improve your own performance before you try to understand others and improve theirs.

The Four Primary Skills

Effective team working seems to require four primary skills:

- directing
- implementing
- learning and
- integrating.

I call these primary since they seem to underpin long-term success in team settings. These, in turn, are supported by the secondary skills needed for specific tasks, eg problem solving — but first let us consider the primary skills.

Directing No group can operate effectively without direction. To be able to direct, a team member or leader must have the ability to articulate targets and priorities for the team. The skill of directing ensures that the team keeps its attention firmly fixed on what it is trying to achieve. The skill of directing also enables the team to allocate its resources to the task in the most effective manner.

The members with this skill are concerned with questions such as 'What are we trying to achieve?' 'What is the best use of our resources?' and 'What should we do first?' Although you might expect the group leader or chairperson to be concerned with these questions, you must recognise that he might not be the best person to answer them — or even ask them! In your team, who asks these questions?

Implementing The members of the team with implementing skills are primarily concerned with doing. They are task-oriented, anxious to make progress, willing to put their energies behind the leader and ready to accept the leader's direction. The skills of implementing also include attention to detail in some members — a high interest in ensuring that the standard of the work is of the highest order and that no 'i' is left undotted or 't' uncrossed.

Implementing skills lead members to ask questions such as 'What do we do now?' and 'Are we sure we have covered everything?' and 'Shall we check that again?'

Learning This skill area is most frequently overlooked in teams. It enables the team to reflect on its experience and adapt its methods and relationships on the basis of what works and what does not work for the team.

Those with learning skills ask the questions 'What is working well and why?' 'Should we change the way we work?' and 'What should we do differently next time?'

This is a key skill, yet it is one which is seldom recognised — worse, when it is noticed, it is often regarded with suspicion! A person with this skill may be looked on as being critical or wanting to change everything! If you have someone with this gift, give them all the support you can — they are essential to team growth.

I shall deal with the skill of integration on page 84.

The Basic Skill Model
We can bring the first three skills together to produce a basic model as shown overleaf.

But a team is more than a group of people with individual skills. In order to form an effective team, the skills of the various members need to be brought together in a way that contributes to the targets and priorities of the team. Thus direction should lead to implementation and implementation should lead to learning. But simply sitting three or more people together who have these skills will not guarantee effective working. Their skills must be linked.

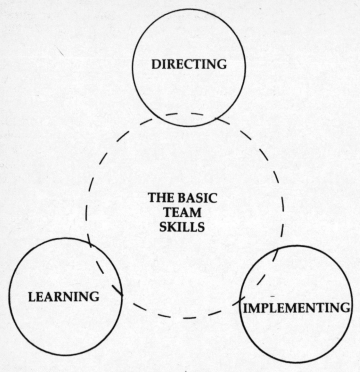

The Basic Team Skills Model

Linking the Skills

Three processes are needed to achieve the full linking of the team's skills:

1   Direction needs to be *translated* into implementation.
2   Implementation needs to be *transformed* into learning, and
3   Learning needs to be *transferred* into new direction.

This can be illustrated as shown opposite.

These linking processes are essential to successful teamwork, and each of the linking processes requires the exercise of skills — the secondary skills. Let us look at these now.

Translating

The translation of direction into implementation requires the group to take the targets and answer the question: 'How can we achieve these targets?' The team's success in answering this question in an effective way depends on how creative and imaginative the team members can be in generating options. 'We could do it this way.' 'Why don't we approach it like this?' 'I've got an idea . . .', etc; and on how critical the team can be in evaluating and judging the various options open to it. 'We cannot do that because . . .' 'The strengths of this approach are . . .' 'What is missing in that idea is . . .', etc. At the heart of the translation process are the skills of *creativity* and *critical thinking*. Without these, the team has difficulty in coupling its vision, direction and targets to appropriate action.

There are many helpful texts on creative thinking. Edward De Bono's book on lateral thinking is perhaps the best known.[7] Creativity requires a positive environment, and in many ways, creative thinking does not sit well beside critical thinking. The team has to help creative and critical thinkers work together.

If these translation skills are missing, the team tends to plunge directly into action which may or may not be appropriate. Many teams are busy on the wrong actions; many teams are successful at the wrong game!

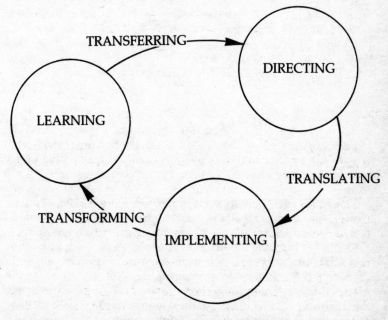

Linking the Three Basic Skills

Transforming

The transformation of experience into learning makes the difference between a team which is successful once and a team which can repeat success at will. Many teams, organisations and churches are dying because they have lost the power of learning. Given a fixed situation, they can perform well, but they are unable to cope with change. They are unable to learn from their experience. Throughout history, nations and cities have fallen because they were unable to innovate and adapt to new technology — chariots, siege engines, long-bows, gunpowder and guerilla warfare.

Two key skills enable action to be transformed into learning; these are the skills of awareness and review. *Awareness skills* are the skills of sensitivity, being conscious of the contribution and interaction of the members, noticing what is going well and what is not, noting what helps and hinders in the group. But awareness without review is not helpful. The observations of the member who is skilled in awareness must be made available to the whole group if learning is to take place.

Review skills are those which ensure that the group's actions and experiences are always open to observation and assessment. 'Hold on, can we just make sure that we are on course?' 'We seem to be spending a lot of time on this — I wonder why that is?' etc.

Once again we touch on skills that are often devalued. 'What's the use of review? — we have finished!' Others will be defensive over the suggestion to review, conscious of the fact that their own behaviour was not as constructive as it might have been, but a regular review will improve their performance!

Transferring

Learning is deemed to have taken place when an individual or a team can behave in a new way, as required. To be able to use learning requires two key skills: conceptual skills and linking skills.

Conceptual skills involve the ability to take pieces of information and bring these together to form a whole, a completeness — a concept. When a group meets, much learning is possible — learning about how people work and how they relate; about feelings; about what happens when people try to work together. Someone with conceptual skills will be able to fit many of these lessons together and create a proposal to apply the learning to the team's targets and priorities. If you have conceptual skills, you will find understanding of this book much easier than if you have to take and apply each piece of advice in isolation.

Linking skills have to do with taking ideas, experiences and lessons from one situation and applying them to another, eg using practices and skills from the work place in, say, the church setting. This could mean transferring the thoroughness of the work place into the church and the enthusiasm of the squash court to the deacon's court!

Integrating Team Skills — The Developed Model
Bringing all these together gives us the developed model as shown:

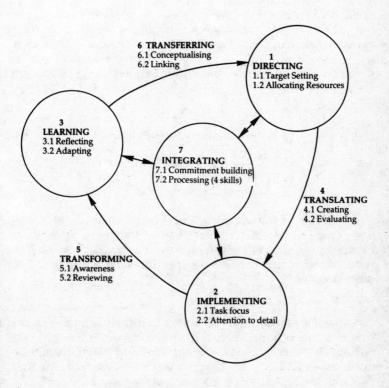

Team Skills: the Developed Model

The area in the centre, where all three basic skills overlap, is the area of integration. Here the aim is to create harmony and unity within the team — creating balance and an interdependence between the members and their contributions. The two skills needed for effective integration are those of *process management* and *commitment building*.

Process Management

We have dealt with commitment building in Chapter 3. While commitment building helps the team maintain its spirit of unity and climate of support, process skills allow the group to deal with interpersonal issues, with the interaction of people. Let us examine this now, for *Team Spirit* is about people working *with* people.

Human relations would be a lot better without people! However, in team settings, at the heart of all teamwork, are our relationships. In a team, we are truly 'people who need people', but the fact that we need them is no guarantee that we will be able to work with them! With conflict on all levels of our society, it seems that we are losing the skills that help people work together. What are these skills? In the context of the team, four are vital. They are —

— listening skills

— communicating skills

— empathy skills, and

— influencing skills

The advent of the television and — more recently — the video and computer as entertainment has undoubtedly reduced our capacity to interact effectively, if only because these media have reduced the amount of time we spend looking at and talking to other people.

Listening skills It has often been observed that God gave us two ears and one mouth because listening is more important than talking! But listening skills are not easily acquired, mainly because they require us to exercise mental discipline. Think for a moment about what happens when you speak. First of all, you begin with an introduction, eg 'Well, I agree with what you have said, but what I would just like to say is . . .', then you move on to say what is really important. Finally you close off with a statement of this kind: 'So, this is really what I feel is important, and I think the group should take note of my position — not that I am trying to be obstructive.' In effect, the real meat of your statement is sandwiched between two quite irrelevant statements. These statements may, in fact, be very long indeed, while the 'meat' might be quite thin! Now consider what happens when you are listening:

1. You hear the opening words, and, in this case, you will respond to the words 'agree' and 'but'. Immediately, your mind goes off and begins to prepare a response to that 'but'.
2. Your mind is now working on the opening words just at the critical point where the speaker's real thought is voiced.
3. You may have missed the real point, but now you know what to say, so you can pay full attention again!
4. The speaker is winding up and has your full attention, but has nothing to say!

This can be illustrated graphically by tracing the importance of the content of the speaker's message and the level of attention of the listener against time.

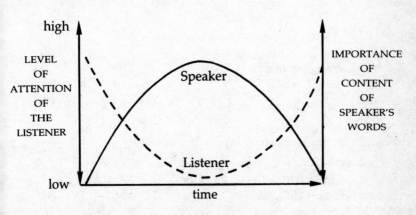

Why We Fail to Hear What Is Said

The reason why we fail to understand is all too obvious to see!
    How good a listener are you? Score yourself on the following 20 questions.

86

ARE YOU A GOOD LISTENER?

ATTITUDES	Almost Always		Occasionally		Almost Never
1 Do you like to listen to other people talk?	5	4	3	2	1
2 Do you encourage other people to talk?	5	4	3	2	1
3 Do you listen, even if you do not like the person who is talking?	5	4	3	2	1
4 Do you listen equally well whether the person talking is man or woman, young or old, black or white?	5	4	3	2	1
5 Do you listen equally well to friend, acquaintance and stranger?	5	4	3	2	1

ACTIONS
When talking to, or listening to someone —

6 Do you put what you have been doing out of sight and out of mind?	5	4	3	2	1
7 Do you look at the speaker?	5	4	3	2	1
8 Do you try to ignore the distractions about you?	5	4	3	2	1
9 Do you smile, nod your head, and otherwise encourage the speaker to talk?	5	4	3	2	1
10 Do you think about what is being said?	5	4	3	2	1

COMPREHENSION

11 Do you try to understand what the speaker means?	5	4	3	2	1
12 Do you try to understand why the speaker is trying to communicate?	5	4	3	2	1

13	Do you let the speaker finish what he is trying to say?	5	4	3	2	1
14	If the speaker hesitates, do you encourage him to go on?	5	4	3	2	1
15	Do you restate what is said to check your understanding?	5	4	3	2	1

EVALUATION

16	Do you withhold judgement about ideas until the speaker has finished?	5	4	3	2	1
17	Do you listen, regardless of the manner of speaking and choice of words?	5	4	3	2	1
18	Do you listen, even though you anticipate what the speaker is going to say?	5	4	3	2	1
19	Do you question the speaker in order to get a full explanation of the ideas?	5	4	3	2	1
20	Do you ask the speaker to define technical or unfamiliar words he uses?	5	4	3	2	1

Your Total Score _____

Assessment

If you scored less than 50, I am surprised anyone bothers to include you as a member of a team! You really must pay particular attention to this chapter. If you scored between 50 and 70, you are in danger of losing contact with those in your team, but your interpersonal relationships will improve as you apply the ideas in this section.

Over 70 and you are a good listener. Keep it up! Whatever your score in total, pay special attention to those areas which you rated three or less.

Here then are 10 commandments for listening. You will need to practise them. Today's world, if it has trained us at all, has trained us in one-way communication – giving! We must work hard at receiving.

88

The Commandments for Listening

1 Do be prepared to work hard at listening.
2 Do keep an open mind.
3 Do beware of hearing only what you want or expect to hear, and don't make assumptions about what people are going to say.
4 Do listen to *how* things are said, but don't spend your time mentally criticising the way a contribution is being presented.
5 Do withhold judgement or evaluation until the entire point has been presented.
6 Do ask for clarification if you have not understood.
7 Don't be afraid to admit you 'switched off' for a minute or misheard.
8 Don't think about *your* next contribution while another person is talking.
9 Don't interrupt, and don't finish people's sentences for them – you could be wrong.
10 Don't react emotionally to personal 'red-flag' words.

Communication skills Listening is only one aspect of communication. Many other signals are given and received apart from the words that we speak. This is particularly so in a team, where you are in close proximity to others. In any dialogue more than 75% of the communication is visual, not verbal, as most people think! In the many public seminars that I conduct on the subject of team building, I give to the delegates an extensive manual covering the material of the presentations, but I give it out at the end of the seminar. The reason for this is so that during the sessions, delegates will look at me as I speak and not at their notes. To follow the notes would mean that less than half of what I wished to communicate would reach the delegates.

Look at the diagram opposite, which shows the main components of the communication process.

So now you know why it is so difficult to communicate! Non-verbal communication has become a rich field of study in recent years. It seems that our actions do speak louder than our words. Seven out of the 10 components in communication have nothing to do with speech!

Think for a moment about the silent signals that you give each time your team meets. How do you dress for the team meeting – formally or informally? – neatly or untidily? Will the other members recognise that meeting with them is important to you by the way you have prepared yourself? This appearance component is quite critical in interviews and in teams where there are unwritten rules of dress.

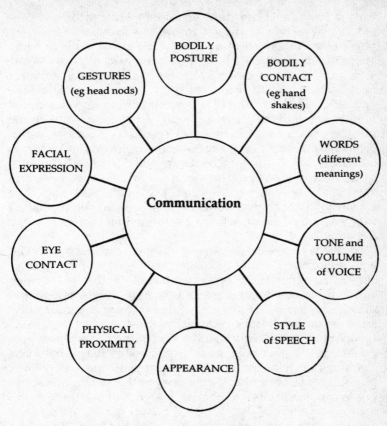

Communication Components

The eyes are the windows of our souls. In our eyes, for those who can read them, are messages which drown our words and outshine the most dazzling of smiles. We can control our mouth, but our pupils contract and dilate without our bidding and signal our appreciation or rejection of those around. Eye contact is perhaps the single most important non-verbal message we give. Too often, our warm smile stops at our mouths and our cold eyes tell the real message. What does your face do for your communications? Does it reinforce them or betray them? If you want to communicate — look at your listeners. If you want to hear, look at the speaker!

Body language has been made a popular subject by (among others) Desmond Morris,[8] but it has been used in management training and team selection for many years.[9] Physical proximity — how close you stand to people — carries with it messages of trust or suspicion. Next time you are in a large store or office block, take a ride in the lift to the top floor and watch the phenomenon of social distance at work. Social distance is the space that people prefer to keep around them. With strangers, as in a lift, it is surprisingly large. Given the opportunity, most people stand two to three feet from you − normally on the opposite side of the lift! Try it. Acquaintances stand closer, and friends are touching. How close do you stand or sit with the members of your team? The Teach Yourself book on non-verbal behaviour[10] shows that the areas we allow friends and relatives to touch vary according to the nature of the relationship. Physical contact is a powerful reinforcer of words. If you want to show pleasure, concern, affection, trust, etc, these may all be conveyed by touch. No words need be spoken, but in addition to words, physical contact creates a communication not readily forgotten.

For the next week, make a note of those who touch you. You will be surprised! Many companies train their employees actually to make contact during communication with customers, eg airline hostesses, hotel receptionists, shop assistants, etc. Research has shown that physical contact increases trust, security, and a sense of well-being and reduces stress!

Social norms vary from country to country, but as it is appropriate, get close to your team − physically! It will help you communicate. However, do remember that for some people physical contact is embarrassing or even threatening. Be sensitive to people's needs.

Empathy is another key skill which helps communication. You may have in your circle of friends a special person who always seems to know the right thing to say in difficult situations, who always seems to understand how you feel and know the words or actions which help. What this person is using is empathy − the skill of being able to communicate their understanding of your situation and feelings. This is a tremendously important skill to have in your team.

Empathy is the ability to care for another person. One writer puts it this way:

> To care for another person, I must be able to understand him and his world as if I were inside it. I must be able to see, as it were, with his eyes what his world is like to him and how he sees himself . . . I must be able to be with him in his world in order to sense from 'inside' what life is like for him.[11]

Empathy is not saying, 'I understand'; it is showing by your words and actions that you do understand! To develop your skill in this key area of empathy you should –

1   Pay close attention to what the other person is saying and how he is saying it.
2   Put yourself into the other person's shoes and give a response that shows you know what it feels like to be there.
3   Listen to the emotion in the voice and the words of the other person.
4   Make no judgement about the other person's situation or problems; concentrate on understanding.
5   Give time to other people. You cannot empathise if you are in a hurry, or your mind is running on to your next meeting or meal.

This last instruction is important. You can do damage to your relationships and to your team members if you rush the process of relationship building. For those interested in developing their skills in this area, I can recommend Gerard Egan's *The Skilled Helper*.[12]

Working with people requires you not only to be able to communicate, understand and empathise; it requires you to be able to influence.

Influencing skills You must never forget that no matter how good a team becomes, it is still made up of a number of individuals. A team has no life of its own; it only exists because different people have given some of their life to it. Each member of the team brings to it not only his own skills, but his own dreams and priorities.

To live effective lives, you must have a personal vision about your future – what you want, what is important to you and how you are going to achieve your targets. I have dealt with this fully in the book *Seconds Away!*[13] Others around you and in your team also have such targets and priorities, and it is likely that they are different from yours. As we have seen earlier (page 47), the team as a whole also needs targets and priorities. Sometimes these priorities – yours, others' and the team's – will be mutually exclusive. You will not be able to go to an aerobics class if the team holds its next meeting on Friday, and Friday is the only day that Jean can come to the team meeting this week. So what has to change? Whose priority will not be met? The answer to this question depends on who has the best-developed influencing skills.

How do you influence people? On a recent fishing trip with my family, our attention was attracted by a bird in obvious difficulty some 50 yards away from us on the loch. We turned the boat towards the duck. Its wing was damaged, and as we approached it made pitiful attempts to lift off from the water, but only succeeded in creating a lot of noise and spray. Nevertheless it began to make some very undignified progress away from us. Even with the outboard motor on full throttle, the bird kept the distance between us and it constant. After about five minutes it stopped, turned and took a good look at us, then with all the grace of a natural flier took off in the direction of the distant shore! We had been victims of the 'broken wing' strategy, used by a number of birds to lure danger away from the nest and young! What had appeared to be weakness was, in fact, a very powerful influencing tactic — the lame duck approach. Weakness and dependence is one of a number of styles used in influencing. Here are some others — taken from the world of unprotected species! Do you recognise yourself?

1   *The greater crested rank puller* This creature is always seen at the best restaurants, parties and resorts. It is fairly common in large organisations, but is seen to best effect on its own among the less well connected and drabber species of the country. Its characteristic strut can be spotted from the furthest side of even the largest rooms, and there is no mistaking its call which begins with: 'When-I-was-talking-to . . ' The only way to catch the greater crested rank puller is to take with you a copy of *Who's Who* and wait for the rank puller's call; a quick reference will give you several names of higher status. Simply drop these names and the bird will be eating out of your hand in a few minutes! The rank puller's influence is quite harmful to other birds, since it tends to dazzle them and lead them into dangerous situations they would otherwise have avoided.

2   *The higher calling bird* This is one of the less common birds of the country. It is hard to spot, since it can often be confused with its much noisier relative, the *prejudiced bigot bird*. The higher calling bird has some very distinctive habits. When in danger of losing an argument, it invariably will attempt to raise the level of debate by at least 200 feet, and there are reports of sightings at the amazing altitudes of 'the meaning of life' and even 'the origin of evil'. One of the richest experiences so far reported is of one continuous sighting which began with an encounter over the colour of a church door, escalated through the symbolic significance of blue in the Judaeo-Christian tradition, and finally, came to rest on a one-litre tin of Woolworth's discount egg-shell varnish. Attempts are being made to reintroduce the higher calling bird to more areas of the country, since one of its positive influencing features is that it can often cause other birds to obtain a better perspective on a local problem. This is very helpful.

3 *The far-sighted peeper* Almost extinct now is the far-sighted peeper, fabled for its ability to see beyond the current problems, it can now only be seen occasionally among groups of birds who are at sea. The peeper is reputed to be able to fly much better in the dark. Experiments with confused birds tend to confirm this, and certainly the bird's capacity to describe distant positions seems to provide inspiration for others. It is puzzling to explain the decline of such a prized species, but it may have something to do with the spread of the short-term feed-back falcon.

4 *The short-term feed-back falcon* The influence of this predatory bird has increased dramatically in recent times. It thrives in competitive habitats and is only content when it is in complete domination of its terrain. It is unique in the world of birds in that it is self-generating. Only one bird needs to be introduced, and soon there will be flocks of them. Their behaviour pattern is quite distinctive, too. They preen themselves in public; in fact, this bird is best observed if you can get together a bus load of admirers. Their call, 'Who's-a-pretty-boy-then?' is quite easy to mimic. Unfortunately, as we have seen, its impact on other species is very destructive. It attacks any other bird which competes for territory, food, position or air space. Bird lovers concerned with the problems that accompany an infestation of the feed-back falcon should note that the most successful method of dealing with them is to ignore them. Two meetings without an answer to their call, 'Who's-a-pretty-boy-then?' seems to be as much as the bird can stand before it is forced to move on in search of more feed-back.

5 *The long-taled warbler* One of the most harmless, yet frustratingly elusive of our wildlife heritage is the long-taled warbler. The warbler is known for its longevity; in fact, no young birds have ever been found. Its most distinctive feature is its capacity for singing long melodious tunes, never less than 20 minutes long, and always more than 20 years old. There are some recurring themes, no matter where the bird sings. These sound like: 'When-I-was-young' or 'We-never-did-it-that-way-before'. Its approach to conflict is fascinating. When faced with any competitor, it begins to sing. Before long the other birds have fallen asleep, leaving the long-taled warbler to make what it wants of the situation.

6 *The double-jointed diver* There are few sights more inspiring than a flight of these magnificent creatures in formation. No matter what the conditions, these birds always seem to be able to get their act together. This is perhaps due to their anatomical peculiarity of being completely double-jointed. They can assume any configuration and may twist themselves into any position in attempts to keep the team together. It would seem

that this bird's overwhelming desire to conform may eventually be its downfall. Conflict is totally unknown among the double-jointed divers. When threatened, they close ranks and dive together, often from great heights, into the sea. Their future is in some ways tied up with the far-sighted peeper, which used to be seen flying in front of these plummeting formations. Increasingly, with the decline of the far-sighted peeper, there are reports of flocks of divers hurtling to their destruction on wet roads and garden ponds. This would be a great loss to our natural fauna, yet who will ever forget that haunting call, 'Unity-unity-unity'?

7 *The lesser-brained shoveller and the progress-making pecker bird* So called because of its ability to push around birds of lower intelligence, the lesser-brained shoveller is often mistaken for its cousin the progress-making pecker bird. Although they have similar habitats and their nests and eggs are identical, the big difference is in their social behaviour in the flock. The shoveller will single out the weaker birds, displaying before them and seeking to mate with the dimmest of the flock. This is the exact opposite of most other species, of which the pecker is a classic example. In the case of the progress-making pecker, the male is particularly willing to please. He goes to any lengths to gain agreement. Courtship is long and steady. The hen bird is not easily influenced and therefore the progress-maker will put great effort into all that he does. He may build as many as six or seven nests before coming to a situation that suits his chosen partner. This bird can often be seen sitting on his nest in late autumn or winter. His chosen site will be immaculate, but the eggs are always late and rarely hatch.

New species of influencing birds are being discovered daily, so keep a look-out for them!

Although we can look at influencing with tongue in cheek, influencing is serious business. Ask any consultant, counsellor, teacher or advertiser. We are open to the hidden persuaders every waking moment, and perhaps never more so than when we are in our team. 'How do you influence others?' is one question, but another of perhaps even greater importance is the question: 'How are you influenced?' The answer is that you are probably influenced by the same factors that you use to influence others. Are you influenced by −

− someone's willingness to help you?

− rank, or status, or contacts?

− intellectual ability?

    — the description of something to be achieved which is both desirable and challenging?

— power?

— the opportunity to win?

— praise?

— tradition?

— the need to avoid confrontation or conflict?

— a logical argument?

It is important for you to recognise the real thing that influences you. Other people have no doubt made a special study of you. Now is the time to understand yourself.

As we come to the end of the chapter on skills, let us take a look at your own array of skills. Where are you strong? Where are your deficiencies? When you can answer these questions, then and only then can you begin to work to build your own and your team's skills.

Assessment of My Own Skills

Consider your skills in the light of this chapter. Place a tick in the appropriate column.

SKILLS		MY ABILITY		
		Weak	Fair	Strong
1	**Directing**			
1.1	target setting			
1.2	allocating resources			
2	**Implementing**			
2.1	task focus			
2.2	attention to detail			
3	**Learning**			
3.1	reflecting			
3.2	adapting			

Continued

SKILLS		MY ABILITY		
		Weak	Fair	Strong
4	**Translating**			
4.1	creating			
4.2	evaluating			
5	**Transforming**			
5.1	awareness			
5.2	reviewing			
6	**Transferring**			
6.1	conceptualising			
6.2	linking			
7	**Integrating**			
7.1	**Commitment building**			
7.2	**Processing**			
7.2 A	listening			
7.2 B	communicating			
7.2 C	empathy			
7.2 D	influencing			

Summary

This section, perhaps more than any other, emphasises just how difficult it is to produce really effective teams. The skills identified here, both primary and secondary, are often not available, or developed, or recognised, or used in teams.

In later sections, we will consider how the deficiencies of skill may be identified and overcome, but before we move on, you should set yourself a target. Develop one skill in which you are weak. Check your assessment list. Which skill will you work on?

TEAM DEVELOPMENT

Chapter 6

Change is (ironically) one of the *permanent* features of our world, whether it happens in the cycle of the seasons or in the structure of our cities or in the skills needed to acquire and maintain employment. We are all subject to change. Left unmaintained, all man-made structures tend to decay, malfunction, or break down. The team is no exception.

In his work on teams, John Adair[1] describes three interlocking needs in group life, **shown overleaf.**

These three overlapping concerns are the core responsibilities of the group leader. You will see that his use of the term 'maintaining the team' highlights the need to care for and repair the relationships within the team. Each of the elements in Adair's model − task, team and individual − **represents needs which if** not met, will reduce the team's efficiency.

Adair suggests that effective leaders and their teams are able to meet and balance the sometimes conflicting demands of these three elements. Other writers have developed Adair's concepts, but his initial insights have remained basically unchallenged.

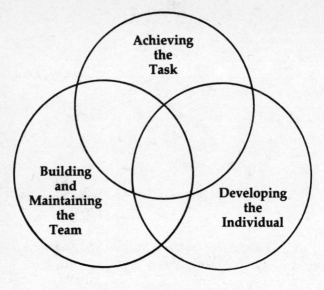

Adair's Interlocking Needs of a Team

The Need for Balance

The 'needs' of the three circles are described in differing words and with differing emphasis by various writers, but the following summary captures the main points – and surprise! surprise! – you need not have studied the literature to recognise them.

To be successful a team must be able to meet the following needs:

Individual Needs (Your Own and Others')

– to be accepted by the leader

– to be valued by the leader

– to be able to contribute to the task

– to know what is expected in relation to the task

– to be part of the team

– to know what is expected of you by the team.

Think for a moment about your team. These are your needs, are they not? Are they being met?

Task Needs

— to set clear targets for the task

— to set standards of performance

— to make full use of the resources

— to clarify responsibilities

— to ensure that members' contributions are complementary

— to achieve the set targets and standards.

Can you honestly say that your team meets these requirements? What can you do to improve its performance?

Team Needs

— to know and respond to the leader's style and vision

— to feel a common sense of purpose with the members

— to have a supportive climate

— to grow and develop as a unit

— to have a sense of corporate achievement

— to have a common identity.

It is unlikely that a team will have these needs in correct balance all of the time; in fact it is more likely that there will be an imbalance most of the time! A team is not static — it is dynamic. It has different needs at different times in its life. Consider what happens when a group of people get together for the first time.

Phases of Team Development

The Individually Oriented Phase

Picture a new team. It has not worked together before; members are not familiar with one another's strengths and weaknesses; they are not sure whether they will be accepted by or enjoy working with this group. Already, before a word has been spoken, the individual members have made assumptions about and judgements upon the other members — his hair, her skirt, his shifty eyes!

Individual needs and concerns predominate. Modifying Adair's circles somewhat, we could represent this group thus:

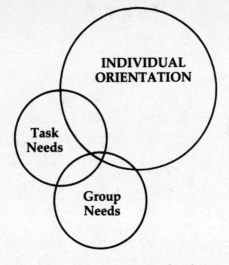

Individual Concerns Predominate

In such a team, whether the team works well or not is of little concern to any of the members; even the team leader may be overly concerned with his performance and acceptance by the group. In such a situation, the needs of the task and the group cannot be met, and the group will not function well.

So what can be done to reduce the concerns of the individuals about acceptance and status? It is probably true to say that it is impossible to avoid this phase. It happens in all new groups. It also applies when a new member joins the team. For a time, the new member will be driven by his personal need for acceptance by the team. However, this phase of a group's development can be shorter if the leader —

1 spends time with each member before the group first meets, or with each new member before he joins the group.
2 finds out about the member's strengths beforehand and introduces the new colleague with a reference to her abilities.
3 states clearly what is expected of the team as a whole and the members as individuals.
4 creates a relaxed, informal atmosphere for the first meeting.
5 deals with his or her own needs first.
6 asks each member of the team to state his or her hopes for the group.
7 gives each member of the group a significant task to do on behalf of the group.

8   gives affirmation to each member at every opportunity.
9   does not allow any one member to dominate the discussion,
    and brings all members into the discussion.
10 ensures that each member contributes − or is invited to
    contribute − fairly frequently during the meeting.

Sometimes a group never emerges from the individually
oriented phase, and it dominates the whole life of a group. Such
a group is characterised by low listening, power plays, manipu-
lation, point-scoring, domination, conflict and withdrawal.
Members are not much fun to be with!

The Task-Oriented Phase

Often, in order to escape from the discomfort and embarrassment of the individually oriented phase, a group throws itself
headlong into the task. It is an avoidance strategy; unable to face
the issue of 'Who am I in this group?' the focus is turned on to
'What can I do?'

Task-oriented groups are characterised by high activity. Pre-
dominant concerns are to do with targets. The needs of the
individuals and of the team are neglected:

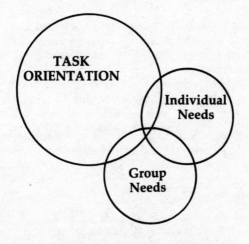

Task Concerns Dominate

If the group is to be short-lived, ie only set up to accomplish a
specific project, this orientation may be the most satisfactory
from the point of view of the task. It is, however, not the
orientation which will create a sense of unity and belonging,
since the individual and team needs are sacrificed to the task.

I remember being called into one company to help identify the source of a rather unusual problem. There had been a spate of nervous breakdowns in the company. The doctor felt that the problem had something to do with the organisation, but could find no link between the people who were showing the symptoms of such severe stress. After some detective work, I discovered that all of the individuals affected were in departments which in the past 18 months had installed new computers or computerised systems! The trail eventually led us to the computer users' service unit. This department was headed by a classic task-oriented individual. He was very intelligent, thoroughly tied up in his work and a hard driver. He always led the joint teams of users and computer specialists and it was his driving, task-oriented style which had put all of these teams under so much pressure. I am happy to say that we were able to help him become more sensitive to the needs of those with whom he worked.

Some guidelines may help you avoid being trapped in the task-oriented phase:

1 Make sure that the task targets are clear and realistic.
2 Put a time-scale on the tasks so that you will know when you have finished. Make sure that you stop when the task is complete.
3 Plan the task, setting timings for each activity.
4 Ensure that for each task target you have at least one team target. A team target would relate, for example, to the quality of the team spirit.
5 Review the progress against the task target and the team target regularly, at least once during each meeting of the team.

These activities will help your team move through the task-orientation phase without too much stress. However, you are not out of the wood yet!

The Team-Oriented Phase
Teams which have been together a long time and have a great desire to maintain their unity may swing to the extreme of neglecting individual needs and even the task in order to maintain an outward show of unity and a supportive sense of harmony. Such a group is more of a play group than a team.

In this phase of the group, there is little or no —

— creative tension, an attempt being made to hold on to everything the team has

   − expressed disagreement, since disonance strikes against the harmony of the team

   − questioning of team norms, since the team is and must be right

− progress or personal growth, since the team holds a high view of its own completeness.

Clearly, the task of the team leader is to steer a balanced course and at various times in the life of the group or in the course of a team meeting to move the team from one orientation to another. For example, he or she must give the team an individual focus as a new member is introduced, push the group into a task orientation when decisions need to be made, and move to a team orientation during the review of a meeting.

What phase tends to dominate in your group? Are you still overly concerned about position in or acceptance by the group? Have you a strong need to achieve, whatever the cost to others in the team? Or are you so concerned about others' feelings that you tend to avoid decisions for fear of creating disharmony? All these are signs of an imbalanced group, a group which has not yet reached maturity.

A Life Cycle

The idea of a mature group brings to mind the concept of a life cycle. This is a helpful way of thinking about team development. In terms of the life of a group, we can identify a number of stages as follows −

1 conception
2 gestation
3 birth
4 growth
5 maturation
6 marriage
7 procreation
8 maturity
9 death, and
10 resurrection.

Each stage of life is different, characterised by different features and needs, and it offers different rewards and threats to the team members. Clearly, as in life, not every team will experience 'marriage' − in the case of the team, this would be a merger − and death is probably some way off for your current team. But as in real life, death usually comes unannounced and is always accompanied by a sense of loss. Let us look at each stage, focusing on its features, experiences, priorities and risks.

Conception

This is the pre-group stage. The group has not met, and perhaps has not even been selected, but nevertheless it is a critical period. In the mind of the conceiver, issues such as –

– the purpose of the group

– the size and nature of the group

– its membership

– its leadership

– its skills, etc

require to be thought through. Whose support is required? How will the ideas be shared? How will the various participants be approached and when? These are the priorities for the progenator. Too often, groups are brought into existence without sufficient thought given to these issues. This is one of the risks of this stage. The world is full of unwanted groups! Without a clear understanding of why a group is needed and of how it will fit into this world and function in relation to it, the creator will be responsible for much unhappiness. Let me illustrate.

A European company was having difficulty in co-ordinating its acitivities in the various countries in which it operated. There were many reasons for this, not least of which was that the **companies did not want to be co-ordinated, they wanted to be** able to operate autonomously in their own countries. In some desperation, the headquarters established a central co-ordination team. This team was made up of members taken from each of the six countries. Each member was relocated in Brussels. Not one of the six wanted to live there; none of them agreed with the principle of co-ordination, and each was given a three-line description of what he was expected to do. You can imagine the disarray that I encountered when I was asked to help!

If you ever have the opportunity to set up a team, make sure that it is well conceived.

Gestation

The larger the creature, the longer the period of gestation, so that in an elephant, the time has extended to 18 months. A group should lie somewhere between the 9 weeks of a cat and the 18 months of an elephant! And of course, the larger the group, the longer should be the gestation period. This, I am afraid, rarely happens. Groups are put together hastily, and the case for the existence of many of them is a bit thin! If there is any way to do a job without using a group, then do not burden yourself and others with an additional complex set of relationships. If, however, a team is the best or only way to do things, then during this time, attention must be given to the objectives and role of the group. These should be written down. The tasks and priorities should also be spelt out and approval should be obtained from other groups in the system to whom the new team will report or with whom it will be required to work.

It is not wise to set every detail in concrete before the team meets. There must be an opportunity for the team members to influence the activities of the new team; thus, during this period, formative ideas might be tested with potential group members.

This is a delicate stage in the life of a group. Many groups naturally, or by external forces, abort during this time, either because the teams were badly conceived or because of opposition from existing groups or individuals.

Gestation is the time to ensure that what has been begun is nourished and protected and allowed to develop naturally. Do not rush it; take your time. Seek advice and support from all those around, particularly those who will be key to the future — the members themselves.

Birth

The launch of a new team is a cause for celebration. From the very start, the leader should be setting the tone of enthusiasm, confidence and a sense of belonging. This means giving the birth significance. Not only must the team feel that it is right, but the people around must feel that this is the right team.

Marking the birth can be done in many ways, by a speech, by a dinner, by publicity, by a gift or by a significant act on the part of the team leader. Jesus quietly selected his team, one here, one there; but having got them altogether, he publicly and dramatically declared to them and the world that this team meant business. The result of the miracle of the water into wine was that his team believed in him.[2]

The early days of the team's life are critical. As the new-born baby is naturally completely selfish, so — as we have seen — the new team is very individually oriented.

Unfortunately, teams may be born damaged. A frequent occurrence in industry is that the best membership is not available or that members are not able to be released in time for the birth, so the team begins life without full resources, and imbalanced. Worse perhaps is the experience of having one or more members forced upon the team for 'political' reasons: 'It won't look good if you don't involve Sam.' Team life is difficult enough without a handicap from the start.

Nevertheless there is joy in working with teams that have had a bad start in life and are determined to succeed and who, with a little help, can achieve great things.

Growth

A new team can make rapid progress. Its performance as a unit will be quite unrecognisable at the end of its first year. This will not continue indefinitely. A new baby doubles its weight in the first four months. If it weighed eight pounds at birth and continued to grow at this speed, by the time it was five it would weigh over two hundred tons! So continued rapid growth is not always a good thing.

In the first year of your team's life, there will be a rapid growth in commitment, motivation and skill; consequently, performance will improve. But it will not be plain sailing all the way. There will be times of doubt and confusion and conflict. A study of the experiences of the disciples of Jesus gives many examples of these, so it is important that the team is realistic about its immaturity and learns to live with and laugh at its mistakes.

Numerical growth should be avoided in the first year, unless this was part of the original design. Turnover may be unavoidable, but once again, do not rush to replace the lost member. The team will probably function better short-handed than with a full complement that includes a newcomer.

Maturation

The time taken for groups to come to maturity varies according to size, the style of leadership and the frequency of meetings, etc. A good rule of thumb is *three years!* This figure always calls up disbelief and dismay in teams, yet it is better to be realistic about how long it takes than to be dismayed by lack of progress. It takes you the first year to decide how the team is going to operate most effectively; then it takes you the second year to try this out and to discover that it is not the best way at all! The third year lets you put into practice what you have learned about effective working in the first two years.

Many teams do not have three years — for example, project groups and special-task groups. In these situations, maturity will never be reached. Their life span is designed to be limited, and their death will come with the completion of the task. They will never reach that balanced state where the needs of the individual, the task, and the group are all met. Leaders and members of such groups must therefore ensure that they do not develop unrealistic expectations.

Marriage

The merger of two or more groups is a difficult process. This is true also when individuals, companies or even nations attempt to merge. Mergers can occur in a wide range of circumstances. For example, in the case of two companies or churches, the merger may come from a gradual realisation that neither can survive alone or that a much better opportunity can be pursued by the combining of the resources. In the former, the merger is being forced – a shot-gun wedding! The parties begin with reluctance, and the prognosis for their future is bleak. In the case of two willing partners, both excited about the future, the chances of success are considerably higher. Yet it must be said that mergers are on the whole not good news for teams.

The problems come from the differences in the two groups. Each group will have developed its own way of doing things, its own style of leadership and participation, its own priorities and norms. To merge successfully requires very high levels of commitment and motivation.

Take plenty of time if you are faced with a merger of two groups. The parties should spend time together exploring their expectations of the new arrangement before the actual marriage takes place. Follow again the stages of conception, gestation and birth, for what you are creating is something quite new.

Procreation

In some situations, successful groups need to reproduce themselves in order for their vision to be developed. Again, this results in a new group, so follow through the early stages with care. Often, some members from the original group provide the core of the new group. This can be a difficult time for the parent team, as well as for the members who are being launched off on their own.

The first problem arises when consideration is being given to who should be sent. In a good team, loyalty will be high and no one will want to leave behind the friends and colleagues with whom they have shared so much. The sense of loss can be high and for a time, quite disabling for both the teams.

A second problem arises if the mother team wishes to hang on to its best members. If you intend to set up a new team, put your top performers into it. Give it the best chance of success that you can. Many new teams have failed because the core membership was made up of people who *could* be spared.

A third threat to any new team comes from over-control by the parent group. Attempts may be made to force the norms and priorities of the original group on to the new one. Although there are probably some areas where conformity is important, as much freedom as possible should be given to the young team. It is helpful to agree on these areas before the new group is set up.

Maturity

'. . . the whole body, joined and held together by every supporting ligament, grows and builds itself up in love as each part does its work.'[3] So St Paul describes the successful team — in his context it was a church, but the truth is applicable to groups in any setting. Note that the mature group is made up of competent, committed members who are conscious of the needs of others. This, in a sentence, is what each team should be striving to achieve. Adair describes the properly functioning team as being one in which:

- people care for each other
- people are open and truthful
- there is a high level of trust
- decisions are made by consensus
- there is a strong team commitment
- conflict is faced up to and worked through
- people listen properly
- feelings are expressed freely.[4]

These attitudes and behaviours characterise mature people operating in a supportive environment. They represent the target of all team development. In one way, it is more of a journey than a destination. It is also a choice. Groups do not mature by neglect. The change and decay that is all around is also within. The group that would come to full stature must give attention to its growth. Without this, it will face premature and lingering death.

Death

The end may be dramatic and spectacular, like Custer's last stand or the charge of the Light Brigade. On the other hand, the passing might be silent and unmarked, as in Rosemary Sutcliffe's story of the Ninth Legion which mysteriously disappeared in the mists of the Scottish glens.[5] Whatever the nature of its going, your team will die. It may, in fact, experience many deaths, for death comes in many forms. Each time you lose a team member, part of the team has died; each time you fail to achieve your targets, something is lost that may never be regained. So death need not be the total break-up of the team, although this, too, you should be ready for. Sadly, I encounter many teams which are long dead, although they continue to meet regularly and go through the motions of life, but their vision has gone and as a team they have perished. Recognise when your mission as a team is ending, and give the end a significance. If the team was effective, then reward it. If the team did not perform, then draw lessons from its experience that may be of help to others. The winding up of regiments, administrations and organisations is often accompanied by ceremony and thanksgiving. These activities give significance to those who have served. They also signal the end. They allow the teams to die with dignity; they allow the expression of sorrow, regret and loss and grief; they also allow those involved to put their past behind them and create new visions for the future.

Resurrection

Occasionally teams have a cyclical life pattern, being set up and disbanded according to a set time-table. For example, conferences or sporting events which take place every four or five years may be organised by committees and teams that go through a number of life/death/resurrection cycles.

There are special problems with this experience. First, there is the problem that the environment has changed since the group last met, and those who were together in the previous life may have difficulty coming to terms with this fact. A second problem is that the membership has changed; not all the team members have been resurrected! Once again, the previous members may want to see the good old days back again and may be reluctant to change or adopt new approaches. The third issue is of comparisons; references will be made to 'the way we did it the last time', and the standards not being as high as *we* made them, etc, attitudes which, of course, tend to divide the group. Even when the team is made up of the same membership, the fact that they have been apart for so long inevitably means that views and attitudes will have changed and that problems will arise as a result.

A fourth problem comes from the expectations of those around the team. They expect at least as good a performance as in past years, despite the fact that the budget may be reduced or that costs have risen, etc. How can these problems be dealt with?

One approach is for the team to identify what has changed for the team both within the team and in the environment. This reinforces the fact that it is a different world and a different team. Armed with these insights, the team can then go on to identify what it will have to do differently — more of, less of, new activities, etc. Of all the stages of team development, this is perhaps the most difficult, next to death.

Summary

An understanding of the stages of team development is necessary for the practical work of team building. You now have descriptions of the motivation, skills, structures and activities needed to create and maintain an effective team. In the next section of *Team Spirit*, from Chapters 7 to 9, we shall focus on putting these insights into practice, but before we leave this section, let me ask you a few questions about your own team. You may want to discuss them with colleagues.

1 What are your team's strengths and weaknesses?
2 How is your team structured? Is its structure appropriate to its leadership style, its tasks and the needs of the members?
3 What stage of development has your team reached? What are you doing to prepare it for the next stage?
4 What are the priorities for the development of your team?
5 What action will you take as a result of your answers to these questions?

PART 3
Applying the Skills

Chapter 7

What is required for a team to work effectively? Although commitment is the essential starting point and basic skills are needed for even mediocre performance, what seems to distinguish the effective team from the rest is a core of activities. No matter what the purpose, size, composition or structure of a group, to work well it must engage in:

1 setting targets for its work
2 monitoring its performance
3 promoting and maintaining communication
4 managing any changes within the team
5 consciously developing its members
6 good stewardship of its resources
7 managing its relationships with other groups
8 learning from its experience
9 monitoring and managing its environment, and
10 building its own relationships.

This core of 10 activities provides a basis for teams to engage effectively in their tasks, while ensuring the needs of the team itself, the members, and those in the wider environment, are met. Let us look at each element in the core in more detail.

1 Setting Targets

Teams must have a sense of direction and purpose if they are to survive. This can best be achieved by establishing clear, communicated purposes and targets. Every member of the team should have something to strive for personally, as well as owing allegiance to the common targets of the group. The team should have targets covering the longer term – say up to 3 years – and targets for the coming 12 months. On the day-to-day level, no action should be tackled without a clear understanding of the target or purpose. Why are we doing this? What will be the outcome?

2 Monitoring Performance

Having set and communicated purposes and targets for the team, it is the team leader's responsibility to regularly monitor the performance of the team and provide the necessary feedback for the steering of the team's activities. The word most commonly used in this respect is 'review'. Reviews should be held regularly. No meeting should be closed without a review. All projects should be reviewed. Each member's performance should be reviewed (see Chapter 12, page 176).

3 Promoting Communication

Many teams fail to recognise that communication cannot be taken for granted. It does not happen naturally – miscommunication is the norm. Communication is not an end in itself but a process designed to aid understanding and commitment. No matter how many times you state a case, if members of the team do not understand or cannot appreciate your views, communication has not taken place. In his book *Whatever Happened to Commitment?* Ed Dayton links communication with community and commitment: 'A group is a community, and if it is to stay together, must be able to share its thoughts and feelings'.[1] This is even more important when it is considering changes.

4 Stewardship of Resources

All of the activities of your team should be conducted with at least one eye on how the resources are being used. The time and skills of the members are irreplaceable and unique, therefore it is important to ask several questions: How well are you using the talent of the team? Are all members contributing? Are all active? Have you passengers? Are your meetings too long? Would members be better employed being elsewhere? It is bad enough wasting your own time, but wasting other people's time should be made a criminal offence! What other resources does a team have at its disposal? Here are the major ones:

A The physical assets − in the form of equipment, finance, buildings, etc.
B The intangible assets − often overlooked. In this area are the more subjective assets such as good will and reputation.
C The team's systems and organisation. The methods by which the team orders its activities are powerful tools to help it achieve its purposes. Unfortunately, they are often taken for granted, accepted as traditions that cannot be altered. In this form, they lose their value as assets and become liabilities − outdated constraints on the life and work of the team.
D The team's relationships − when the climate is supportive and strong, positive relationships flourish. Conversely, strained relationships set up negative dynamics which undermine and sap the strength of the team. The quality of the relationship determines the quality of the communications, the roles of the members, and the degree of satisfaction experienced. Good relationships take time to build, but can be destroyed in minutes.
E The team's identity − the team that does not know who or what or why it is soon loses its way and its life; whereas the team that is clear about its vision and priorities stays together and is successful. Note how after the Crucifixion, the disciples of Jesus began to drift back to their pre-disciple activities: 'I'm going out to fish'.[2] They had lost their sense of purpose.

These are some of the resources available to the team to help it achieve its targets. The resources also need to be enhanced if the team is to be developed. Your resources are your wealth.

Use the checklist on the following page to rate the 'wealth' of your team. Place a tick in the column which best describes your team's state in terms of the assets listed.

5 Management of Change

Change is a natural process. It happens all around, and we have come to accept it as inevitable. All living organisms grow and develop, but teams are not self-sustaining and if left to them-

RESOURCES ASSESSMENT CHECKLIST			
Resource	**Assessment**		
	Deficient	**Adequate**	**Strong**
1 Physical Assets			
Buildings			
Equipment			
Skills			
Money			
Number of members			
2 Intangible Assets			
Good will			
Commitment			
Reputation			
Team spirit			
3 Systems and Organisation			
Financial control			
Planning methods			
Review procedures			
Organisation, authority and structures			
Quality control			
Training methods			
Reward systems			

Resource	Assessment		
	Deficient	Adequate	Strong
4 Team Relationships			
Formal relationship			
Informal relationship			
Communications			
Group relationships			
Climate			
Satisfaction			
5 Team Identity			
Sense of who we are			
Understanding of why we exist			
Knowledge of how we are seen			
Understanding of how we want to be seen			

selves, will break down, decay and eventually die. Teams must be nurtured.

As we have seen already, teams change when membership changes. Teams change as they learn. They change as they mature. They change as they grow tired or receive new life and enthusiasm. All these changes must be managed; that is to say, they must be handled in such a way that moves the team forward in pursuit of its purposes. A change in membership, although always disruptive, can be an opportunity to review and reaffirm the reasons for and vision of the group.

6 Development of Members

Development can be thought of as systematic, planned change designed to alter the characteristics of a person. Team development is, at the personal level, designed to equip members with new skills or capabilities. This is a key task for all teams. The leader should have a clear understanding of what is each team member's priority for development.

Most people find themselves in a variety of group situations throughout the course of a week. In all these situations, the individual has a responsibility to improve the working of that group – even if it means improving only his or her own contribution. Primarily, however, the team leader has responsibility for the development of his own team, for the long-term success of the team depends on his ability to create a stock of talent that can carry the vision and the task of the group into the future. The team is where this development of talent can best take place. Take a piece of paper and make a list of the names of your team members. Alongside each name, write down what you think the development needs are for each member. Begin with yourself!

7 Interaction with Other Teams

The relationships between teams and groups is often more critical to the success of the team than relationships within the team, the latter being more open to influence by the team leader. One target of the team should be to create open communication and harmonious activity with the main teams around it.

These other teams could be functions such as marketing, manufacturing, warehousing and distribution or departments such as sales, orders and dispatch; or church groups such as youth groups, worship groups, community groups, support groups, etc. Much team training fails to take account of the fact that the team has to exist in an environment which is often hostile or at least uninterested.

8 Learning from Experience

There is no group that knows it all. The team that stops learning stops developing and soon stops development. We are our own best tutors, provided we know how to learn from experience. The use of team review material (see page 171) will help the team learn from its experience.

9 Monitoring the Environment

I was conducting a team-building session for a company in Italy. The team of seven was made up of people from four nationalities. Only one member was Italian, and he had just joined the company. After two days, the group was making good progress and was well through the creation of a 10-year strategy for the company, which included a major expansion. Alfonso, the new Italian manager, had been quite active in the early part of the discussion but as the week progressed, his contributions reduced and by Wednesday evening he was clearly withdrawn and anxious. I took an opportunity to raise my observations with him over dinner. 'I wait for the real discussion,' he explained. 'Which one is that?' I asked. 'The closure of the factory, of course!' he replied.

It transpired that on the day the team-building course had begun, he had seen an announcement in the local press (in Italian, of course) about the re-zoning of an area of land as a nature reserve. Not only did that area cover the site of the proposed expansion, but it included part of the existing factory! The management team of expatriates had been unable to monitor its environment effectively! Fortunately, Alfonso's concern was dealt with in time, and the team was able to manage the unexpected development successfully. The team that closes its eyes on the world and looks only inward had better look out!

10 Building Relationships

A team is a working community. In the process of its activities, the interaction of members and the interaction with the world at large inevitably put strain on relationships, which need to be maintained in the same way as do cars.

These 10 activities have been shown to help build strong teams. I have encouraged groups of managers, ministers, volunteers and project teams in many countries to use them. Although some teams have operated successfully for short periods without having to spend time on managing all of these, eventually teams do engage in all of them.

Step-by-step Problem Solving

Now you can take steps to ensure that the 10 core activities are pursued, but in the meantime, work has to be done; the team has to perform. How best to get down to business?

Let me illustrate by reference to an example from the world of climbing. In 1980, the climber Chris Bonnington wrote an account of a climb to the top of Mount Everest in the Himalayas.

His book *Everest the Hard Way* describes a successful team.[3] First, they had a clear target: the challenge was to reach the summit by the hitherto unclimbed South-west Face. Here is the first key to success: know what it is you are trying to achieve.

Second, the Everest team planned out the route in advance. Previous climbs, experience and aerial photographs were all used to plan how many bases and camps would be required. The target was achieved step by step, and step by step the problem was overcome. What steps are required to solve problems in team settings? Surprisingly, problem solving is not difficult when the problem is approached logically. The seven steps in problem solving enable a team to grow daily in its capacity to solve problems; they are:

- Gathering information
- Reviewing the target
- Option finding
- Weighing the options
- Identifying the solution
- Necessary action
- Gaining insights.

Gathering Information

When it comes to problem solving in teams, a major strength of the group is that more minds can be applied to the challenge. Information is power when it comes to problem solving, so time must be given to finding out who knows what about the difficulties. Most of the great scientific and technological achievements of the past decade would have been impossible without the computer, which has given the power of quick information access. The more angles you get on a problem, the easier it will be to solve. This is no new discovery. King Solomon found that the more information he had, the closer he got to real wisdom: 'many advisers make victory sure' was his experience.[4]

I have found in my own work that groups rush into action without taking time to clarify their targets, not to mention gather information! Make sure, then, that each member has an opportunity to contribute information. If possible, make your information visual with an overhead projector or a flip chart.

Reviewing the Target

A thorough data-gathering exercise may alter the target. This is often the case in business, when market research reveals that what the customer wants is not what the supplier thought! So, once the data has been collected, ask yourself: What does this mean for our target? Is the target correct? Can the target be more precisely defined? What new pieces of information are important for us? There is no point wasting time on unimportant problems – or problems which no longer exist.

Option Finding

Creativity is almost a lost art. Our societies have placed so much emphasis on logic that much of our adult population has now little ability in this activity. Edward De Bono has been a pioneer in this field and has encouraged and enabled many adults to regain their strength in creative or lateral thinking. He states: 'Man owes his success to his creativity. No one doubts the need for it. It is most useful in good times and essential in bad'.[5]

At the early stages in problem solving the creative members of the team should be encouraged to lead the option-generating step. Ideas are the food and drink of the team – without them, the progress will slow and the energy diminish as the group struggles vainly to tackle new problems in old ways. Ideas must be listed – must be made visible and recorded so that none is lost. The technique of listing ideas is called 'brain-storming'.

It is important to separate the two steps of finding options and weighing them. It appears that the two processes of creating and weighing (or judging) are carried out in different parts of our brain. The left side is logical and carries out most of the evaluating activity, while the right side handles the process of creativity. The mental processes of creating and judging are very different, and this is one reason why successful teams separate the two steps.

Weighing the Options

You cannot weigh one option against another unless you are clear about what it is you wish to achieve. If your target is imprecise, the weighing step will be difficult, if not impossible. So when disagreements develop as to which is the best option, refer again to the target. As we have seen, the number of people who have good judgement skills are few, so pay particular attention to this step.

To help you in the weighing process, try a ranking procedure.

The checklist below is useful in this context. Evaluate each option against the following criteria, and score it as follows:

> 1—outstanding
> 2—acceptable
> 3—marginal
> 4—unsatisfactory.

CHECKLIST FOR WEIGHING OPTIONS	
Criteria	**Score**
1 Time to implement	
2 Cost of implementing	
3 Ease of implementation	
4 Acceptable to all parties	
5 Sense of 'being right'	
6 Enthusiasm for option	
7 Support from outside the group	
8 Compared with other options	
9 Likely to last as a solution	
10 (Write your own)*	
_____	
_____	

* The group should agree which criteria it will use to weigh its options. The criteria should, if possible, be established at the same time as the target is defined.

Identifying the Solutions

From among the options you have generated you need to find the solution. The weighing will have given you a list of solutions in terms of how well they meet your criteria for success, but producing a list and ranking the options is not the end, the group must be prepared to decide — to commit itself to the necessary action.

How are decisions made in your team? There are a number of approaches, each suitable for different situations, but whatever method is used, the group needs to be clear on how the decision will be made, who will make it, when it will be made and what decision has been made (see Chapter 2, page 34).

Necessary Action

The translation of the chosen solution into action calls for the commitment of those to whom the team assigns the responsibility. Each member involved must be clear about what and when it is needed. Avoid involving more people than necessary. If the action can be carried out by one or two members, it should be. Involvement for involvement's sake is a waste of resources and a sign of an immature team.

Gaining Insights

Every activity is an opportunity to learn how to improve and grow as a team. No major action, no meeting should be regarded as complete until the team has reviewed the performance and agreed on what will be done differently the next time around.

These seven steps will provide your team with a systematic approach to solving any problem or discussing any issue to bring it to a conclusion.

More Than Logic

But there is more to teamwork than logic, just as there is more to climbing Everest than marking out a route. Each stage of an assault relies on different contributions from the team members. In the planning stage, those with the greater knowledge are more heavily involved, while during the actual climb, different team members take the lead according to their expertise or stamina. Is it an ice wall, snow field or glacier? Who has the best technique for cutting out a trail for the rest of the team to follow? Of even greater importance, perhaps – Who has the medical skill, and who is the best cook?! At each stage of the climb, team members are expected to contribute their skill to the task involved. As the climb continues, altitude sickness may take its toll of key members, and the team needs to be prepared to go forward without all its members. In these conditions, great care is needed.

So in your team. You should look for members skilled in each step of the seven activities described in this chapter. Of greater importance, however, is that you should ensure that each member applies his or her skills at the right time. If those skilled in *action* dominate in the early *discussion* part of the task — 'Let's get on, we've talked enough!' — there is a great danger of the team being ill-prepared for later stages.

So the team leader must not only look for strong contributions from specific members at each stage, but also for leadership from the members skilled at each particular stage.

Steps, Contributions, and Relationships

Although bad weather conditions are the main reason for the failure of climbing teams to reach their target, the next most frequent cause of failure is a breakdown in the relationships between team members as conflict grows within the team. Alliances, joint ventures, coalitions and committees can only function effectively when relationships are good. Although conflict can sometimes be creative, sustained conflict always leads to loss for all. I will deal with this in greater detail in Chapter 14.

As your team works together and as members contribute, a series of interactions take place between the members. A contribution from one will result in a response from another, but all members will be affected by the exchange. Feelings will arise in all listeners: support, doubt, concern, anger, etc. Many of these effects pass and are soon forgotten, but some will remain. Not all will contribute to a good team spirit.

The three main streams of activity that need to be managed if your team works well are: the *steps* to the targets; the *contributions* of members, and the *interactions* of members. The first, which I have just described, can be adopted fairly readily by most teams; however, it takes more skill and experience to manage contributions and interactions.

Teams that concentrate too much attention on one activity to the exclusion of the others are less likely to achieve their targets than those that maintain an appropriate balance between the three. It is the third stream which is most frequently neglected. Although the symptoms of neglect are often apparent to all, not many groups invest sufficient time in discussing their feelings or their interaction because such discussion is commonly regarded as a 'waste of time'. Thus the issues get swept under the carpet. It is a sign of group maturity when issues of interaction can be openly confronted and the group members' feelings regarded as the legitimate concern of the team.

The diagram following may help you to grasp the concepts more clearly and also to explain them to others.

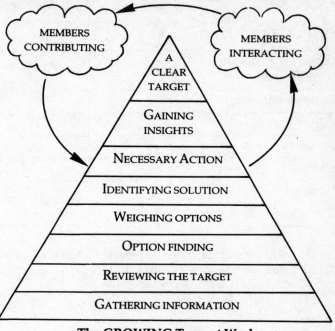

MEMBERS
CONTRIBUTING

MEMBERS
INTERACTING

A
CLEAR
TARGET

GAINING
INSIGHTS

NECESSARY ACTION

IDENTIFYING SOLUTION

WEIGHING OPTIONS

OPTION FINDING

REVIEWING THE TARGET

GATHERING INFORMATION

The GROWING Team at Work

Individual Preferences in Contributions

Our individual gifts, preferences, skills and experiences cause us to behave in characteristic ways. Some people like to explore ideas and possibilities; others like to reflect on what is happening, while others are anxious to come to a quick decision and get on with the work. In fact, individuals in your team probably have preferences to make contributions in two or three of the seven steps.

Consider your team. Overleaf write the names of the two members who are most obviously concerned to contribute at each step of the task procedure. For example, you may put the secretary's name opposite 'information' if he is the one who most frequently draws the team's attention to the need for 'information'; while you may put the treasurer's name opposite 'weighting' if she tends to be evaluative in her contribution.

Step	Member	Member
SETTING TARGETS		
Gathering information		
Reviewing the target		
Option finding		
Weighing options		
Identifying solutions		
Necessary action		
Gaining insights		

How can you encourage these members in their contribution? Are there any members for whom you have listed no contribution? What can you do to discover their talents?

TEAM MEETING

Chapter 8

Most meetings are a waste of time and there must be millions of people attending meetings every day. Meetings have much to answer for! They have variously been described as: 'indispensable when you don't want to do anything'; 'a group of the unwilling, picked from the unfit to do the unnecessary'; 'a cul-de-sac into which ideas are lured and then quietly strangled!' Yet we continue to set them up; we continue to attend, and we continue to be frustrated by them.

In his witty book on meetings, Winston Fletcher observes:

> It is, when you think about it, astonishing how cock-sure most of us are about meetings. We treat them . . . as though they can be mastered without training or guidance or even much forethought. Occasionally, departing from some debacle . . . we suffer a moment's despondency, and briefly face the distasteful fact that we are less intuitively skilful than we had fondly imagined. Then, shrugging it off, we blame our stars rather than ourselves – and rush to the next meeting.[1]

Another writer states that:

> Meetings are what life is all about! Discussions between individuals and groups help us to understand what has to be done, what is being done now and where we may be moving in the future. Despite the importance of meetings, nobody seems to have much good to say about them.[2]

Meetings and Meetings

One reason why we have so much difficulty with meetings is that we fail to distinguish between the types of meeting we are attending. In this chapter, I will deal with some of the most common meetings. We will notice the main differences for the participants and note the conduct of the leader. We shall also note the key skills required. Let us look first at some general rules for running all meetings. These will provide you with some helpful guide-lines.

Running a Meeting

Whether it's a Parent-Teacher Association, a deacons' court, a board meeting or a project group, there are a number of disciplines you should attempt to observe. They are simple, logical, helpful and rarely applied!

1 Inform people well in advance of the time, place and duration of the meeting. This last piece of information is important. There are few things more frustrating than being stuck in a meeting which has overrun its time when you have planned to be somewhere else.
2 Allow as much information, pre-reading and preparation time as possible. This will reduce the amount of briefing and scene setting required during the meeting to bring people up to date.
3 Produce the agenda well in advance. Give members time to think through the issues to be discussed.
4 Start on time. Do not wait for the late comers; even if you are the only one there on time, as chairperson, begin! If you wait for those who are late, you punish those who have taken the trouble to come on time.
5 The first item on the agenda should be the identification of 'Any Other Business'. Ask members to state at the outset if they have other items to be dealt with. This ensures that you are not left with major items of surprise business to deal with in five minutes at the close of the meeting!

6   Divide your agenda into two sections:
   (a) standing items, ie those which always appear — apologies, minutes of last meeting, matters arising, finance, etc, and
   (b) special topics. Never hold a team meeting without at least one special topic (see 8 below). This ensures that the meeting will have some high-lights of interest.
7   Put a target against every item on the agenda, with a deadline. Stick to your time. When the time is almost up for each item, draw attention to the time limit. When the time is up, say so. If necessary, extend the time; but tell the team you are doing so. State the new time allocation and stick to it. If a decision has not been reached at the end of the extension, then you decide or defer the decision till another meeting. Do not allow the discussion to run on.
8   Special topics give the meeting interest and an opportunity for creativity and forward thinking. Avoid having more than three special topics at any one session.
   For a special topic item state:
   (a) the title
   (b) the purpose
   (c) the process to be followed
   (d) any pre-reading/thinking needed
   (e) the time to be allowed, and
   (f) the target of this discussion.

An example of a special topic agenda item is given overleaf. A copy of such a sheet should accompany the agenda for the meeting. The example is taken from a church setting to illustrate that the form is suitable for all environments, not only for businesses.

Two last words about meetings:

9   Review each meeting. Put 'meeting review' on the agenda and perhaps attach a copy of the meeting review form to the agenda (see page 173).
10   Finish on time.

These 10 disciplines will improve your meetings. If you are invited to a meeting in which you are not needed, send your apologies with any ideas or views that you might think the members would find helpful.

Let us now consider some of the different meetings that you may have to attend.

130

EXAMPLE OF SPECIAL TOPIC FORM

Agenda Item 8 – Special Topic

Church Five-year Plan

Purpose: To consider the possibility and value of a five-year plan for the church and to consider how it might be produced.

Process: The Church Administrator will introduce the subject and take the group through the example of St Nicholas' five-year strategic plan. The vicar will then chair the debate.

Pre-reading: Copy of St Nicholas' five-year strategic plan. Come prepared to state in which ways the St Nicholas' approach is useful and what would need to change for us at St Barnabas'.

People: This item on the agenda will be attended by the secretary of St Nicholas', who will answer questions on their experience.

Time: 45 minutes.

Target: To decide whether or not we should progress with the idea of a five-year strategy.

The Board Meeting

Boards usually have a legal status. Their rights, powers and obligations vary from country to country, but basically a board is required to:

1 ensure that the organisation is administered properly
2 elect or remove directors
3 approve the accounts
4 approve the budget
5 approve the appointment of senior staff.

For those readers who are members of a board, I recommend *On the Board* by Geoffrey Mills as essential reading.[3] He illustrates how the legal nature of boards high-lights a number of features of team meetings which are often overlooked in other settings.

First, boards have clear purposes, set down in law and often expanded by the board to suit the local situation.[4] This is critical to their effective working. Many team meetings are held without the members being clear as to the reasons for such gatherings. It is useful to write a set of terms of reference for your meetings. Do you have one? If not, produce one.

Second, boards meet regularly. They must meet at least once a year, but may meet as often as once a month, and dates are put in the diary at least one year in advance. Again, this gives us a guide for other meetings − plan ahead and make sure that the team members are prepared to commit themselves to the time needed.

Third, boards are decision-making bodies and work usually on the principle of a majority vote, provided a quorum is present. A quorum may be only two, so that decisions are not delayed, but each board has its own definition of quorum. How does your team decide? One man, one vote, or by concensus? I sit on the boards of a number of organisations, and each one operates differently. In one, the chairman boasts that he has never had to take a vote in eight years; every decision was made by concensus or not at all.

Fourth, board meetings are expensive. Directors are paid − usually highly − and are often busy executives. So board meetings tend to be short, although this varies. I attend one board which meets twice a year for two-and-half hours each time, while another board meets once a year for five days! Both of these meetings are brisk and cover a lot of ground. The organisation which meets for 5 hours a year is more than 10 times the size of the other! How much time do you really need for your meetings? Try reducing the time 25%.

Board agenda are planned well in advance. Often, there will be set topics on a quarterly or annual basis.[5] This ensures that the larger issues of direction and policy are reviewed regularly. Do you have an annual pattern for your agenda?

Terms of Reference

Most boards are supported by committees. These are useful means of reducing the pressure of work on the main team meeting. Common committees are:

- − finance committee
- − personnel committee
- − policy committee and
- − executive committee.

Each committee is given a set of terms of reference. Here is an example for an executive committee. You will see from its key objective that the executive committee is quite a powerful group.

THE EXECUTIVE COMMITTEE

1 Key Objective
  To act for the board in the periods between the annual board meetings.
2 Composition
  The Executive Committee will be comprised of six board members, including the chairperson, the executive director and four elected members. Five members would be chairpersons of committees and the sixth would be without portfolio. The vice-chairperson would be selected from among the members. Senior managers would be in attendance at meetings, as required.
3 Functions
  a Advise the executive director during the time between board meetings.
  b Take action on matters of business not requiring full board attention.
  c Review strategy and planning materials for presentation to the board.
  d Evaluate annually the performance of the executive director, all board members and committees. Recommend action.
  e Guide the board in a judicious selection and orderly succession of the executive director.
  f Be available to guide the executive director in emergencies, and to meet in emergency session as required.
  g Act in other matters on behalf of the board.
4 Meetings and Locations
  To meet twice a year at Head Office.

This format is very useful. It may be extended by listing the 'key tasks' of the committee.

A fifth useful practice of boards is the spelling out of the role of the chairperson and the board members. This is particularly helpful for new members and for evaluating performance. You will recall that one of the functions of the Executive Committee was to evaluate the performance of members. Here is an example of a role description for a board chairperson. Perhaps you could modify it for use in your own team.

CHARTER FOR THE CHAIRPERSON OF THE BOARD

1 The Key Objective
 To enable the board and its committees to accomplish their key objectives, functions and tasks.
2 Tasks
 a Preside at meetings of the board and its executive committee.
 b Call special board meetings as necessary.
 c Supervise preparation of an agenda for board meetings.
 d Guide the board, so that it acts in the best interests of the company.
 e Establish, maintain and enhance relationships with board members and committee chairpersons.
 f Receive nominations for the membership of committees.
 g Maintain regular contact with the executive director to support and enhance his work. Advise on major organisational changes.
 h Ensure the evaluation of the performance of the executive director.
 i Ensure that the board and committees perform to agreed standards.
 j Ensure that board members are given adequate exposure to the company's operations and are continually updated.
 k Encourage team building among board members.
 l Make periodic visits to the various company locations, and ensure that there is a planned programme for such visits by other board members.
 m Serve as an ex-officio member of all committees. Receive copies of all committee minutes.
 n Ensure the orderly succession of committee members, in consultation with the executive director, through the nominating committee.
 o Ensure the orderly succession of the executive director and his team.
 p Confirm that the minutes of board meetings properly reflect discussions as well as votes, and sign the minutes.
 q Monitor board members who may be given special assignments.
 r Enhance and contribute, where appropriate and possible, to public awareness and public relations on behalf of the company.

Many practices of this chairperson of the board's charter can be usefully translated into other settings, particularly where the team is concerned with the general conduct of an area or activity, be it the golf club, the youth group or a department in an organisation.

Let us move on now to meetings of a more specific nature.

The Problem-solving Meeting

Problems are raised and dealt with during the normal course of team meetings, but occasionally a major decision needs to be taken and requires a specially designed meeting. Here are some tips to follow:

1 Make the meeting special. For example, hold it at a different time or in a different place from the normal meeting.
2 If possible, begin with tea or coffee. This gives people time to relax and also gives time for discovering the positions that members may be adopting towards the problem.
3 Try to create an informal atmosphere, perhaps by removing the tables and asking the team to sit round in a circle.
4 Prepare yourself. Can you clearly describe the problem? Does the team 'own' the problem — ie is it really the team's responsibility? Are you ready to take action?
5 Present the problem to the team positively. Show the problem as an opportunity to improve.
6 Do not blame, accuse or complain. Set out the facts. State clearly what the situation is and, if you know, state what the situation should be. Do not keep cards up your sleeve; if you have information that is relevant, then share it.
7 Involve the team by encouraging open discussion, letting the members talk, and allowing time for options to be generated.
8 Make sure that everyone knows the criteria by which ideas will be judged (see page 122). Always high-light the point at which you feel the team is ready to make a decision.
9 Make sure that the solution agreed specifies the *what, who, how* and *when*.
10 Summarise what has been said and agreed. Check with those who will have to act that they know what to do.

Disagreement

What should you do if you cannot reach a concensus? First, summarise points of agreement and disagreement and stress areas of *agreement*. This is important. It is often helpful to ask each member to state two things they like about what has been proposed. Second, give those in the minority a chance to explain their position, their hopes and fears; and finally, state the situation as a new problem: 'We don't agree — what should we do now?'

The team may choose one of these possibilities:

- They may ask the leader to decide. Be reluctant!
- They may settle for the least disliked solution.
- They may agree to try out a solution for a time and meet again.
- They may exempt some members from commitment for a time.
- They may alternate between plans.

Whatever position the team takes, make sure all know what the next steps are.

Reasons for Failure

There are many reasons why groups will not come to concensus. Here are some common causes:

1   The leader did not present all the necessary information, so the group was unable to fit all the pieces together.
2   The leader tried to railroad discussion so that members would accept his solution, or else he presented several solutions for choice, without allowing time for understanding.
3   The team may be incapable of solving the problem. It may be too large, or the group may have insufficient skills.
4   The group may have been unco-operative on that evening. It may have been a bad day.
5   The group may choose a poor solution that will not work out. Nevertheless the experience can be helpful, provided the team reviews and learns from its failure.
6   There is a time for every purpose and it may be that now is not the time to tackle that problem.

Information

Meetings are a source of information and opportunity to give information. This is one of the key functions of meetings. For some meetings, it is the *only* function. How well does your team meeting operate as a communications centre?

Completion of the following questionnaire will help you evaluate the effectiveness of communication within your own team. Tick the item which applies in your team.

1 From which source do you receive most information?
 − team leader
 − minutes
 − agenda
 − grape-vine

2 Which channels do you use to give information?
 − team leader
 − meeting
 − notice board or intra-office mail
 − grape-vine

3 How often do you feel you have not been 'put in the picture'?
 − never
 − seldom
 − sometimes
 − often

4 Is information hard to come by in the team?
 − never
 − sometimes
 − often
 − always

5 How often do others in the team complain of not being 'in the picture'?
 − never
 − seldom
 − sometimes
 − often

6 How often do you have team meetings?
 − daily
 − weekly
 − monthly
 − annually

7 How often have you found that work you are doing has been or is already being done by someone else in the team?
 − never
 − seldom
 − sometimes
 − often

8 How often have you found that a better briefing would have saved you time or effort?
 — never
 — seldom
 — sometimes
 — often

9 Are you able to communicate at team meetings?
 — always
 — often
 — sometimes
 — rarely

10 How often have you been 'by-passed' in the communication flow?
 — never
 — seldom
 — sometimes
 — often

In my work as a consultant, 'communications' is the most frequent problem raised by managers. Often, it is because of inappropriate structures rather than poor skills. So if your answers do not satisfy you, look again at your structure (Chapter 4).

Meeting Performance

As ever, the conduct of a meeting is in the hands of each member. Success is owed to the whole team, not to the leader or the chairperson. Unless you make your full contribution, the meeting will be less than it otherwise could have been.

We will look further at assessing meeting performance when we deal with evaluation in Chapter 11, but the questions below will help you assess the performance of your meetings. Remember, it is not sufficient to be able to assess performance; you must also apply what you know to improve performance!

1 Write down two or three words or phrases that describe your team meetings.
2 Write down two or three words or phrases that describe how you feel after your team meetings.
3 Are there discernible structures to your team meetings or do things just happen?
4 Do your team meetings progress smoothly, or is there much back-tracking, side-stepping and digression?
5 Are the objectives of the meetings clear?
6 Are the objectives regularly achieved?

7 Is there usually agreement about what is decided?
8 Is the quality of listening high?
9 Are the contribution rates of members about equal, or do some members dominate?
10 Are the meetings adequately controlled?

Summary

In this chapter we have considered some of the principles that underlie the conduct of good team meetings. In summary, a good team meeting —

- has a clearly defined purpose
- is disciplined and structured
- allows for participation
- accommodates success and failure
- allows for communication, and
- provides data for an improved performance at the next meeting.

What ideas have you gleaned from this chapter that might improve the functioning of your team meetings? Write three of them here:

1 _____

2 _____

3 _____

Where better to end a chapter on teams than with a quote from the most powerful chairman of this century? 'If we have a correct theory, but merely prate about it, pigeon-hole it and do not put it into practice, then that theory, however good, is of no significance'.[6]

WHEN THE TEAM WORKS WELL○○○○

Chapter 9

It was finished! We looked around at the faces of those we had
worked so closely with for six months. We saw eyes filled with
emotion. None of us could speak as we embraced and held each
other until the moment had passed. This was the experience of a
team of which I was part − a team that had worked well. Such a
reaction to success is one of the joys of team-work; it is by no
means uncommon.

> I looked at Tensing and in spite of the balaclava, goggles
> and oxygen mask all encrusted with long icicles that con-
> cealed his face, there was no disguising his infectious grin
> of pure delight as he looked around him. We shook hands,
> and then Tensing threw his arm around my shoulders and
> we thumped each other on the back until we were almost
> breathless. It was 11.30 am.[1]

It was also May 29th, 1953 and the place was the top of Mount
Everest!
    When was the last time you experienced these feelings in your
team?

High Morale

Such great 'highs' may not come often since they usually accompany great achievements, but the team that works well is rewarded by a high degree of satisfaction. Have you seen the emotions on the trainers' bench at the end of the World Football Cup Final? Or the invasion of the pitch at the end of a home-win cricket test match? These are public manifestations of the feelings which accompany outstanding success. But another feature of success that is more permanent than the ecstasy of triumph is high morale. High morale is the product of an environment in which people are *clear about their purposes and about the results to be achieved*. They must also be confident in their ability and work together in harmony. How then can you create high morale?

Clear Purposes and Key Tasks

We have already seen how important it is for each member of the team to know his position and his priorities (see Chapter 3). Each member should have a position description, and although this takes time to produce, it is an important element in the formula for high morale. The job description gives a sense of direction to the individual member. It ensures that the leader is doing her job, and the team members are doing theirs, in full understanding of the delegated responsibility and authority of each. The team is geared for successful achievement, and uncertainty is minimised. In the knowledge that her people are achieving their short-term targets, the leader can do the long-term planning and creative thinking so needed for continuous growth and a clear sense of purpose.

Surprisingly enough, high morale does not mean that your team is always successful, but only that it is (at least) successful in priority areas. By 'priorities' we mean the targets we have chosen to put first.

Each role in the team is established to carry out a few specific and key tasks. These bring the vital results, achievement of which dramatically influences the success of the team, and where failure is disastrous. Of the many results any role could produce, the key tasks are the 20% that determine 80% of the team's successes and effectiveness. All team members must understand what their key tasks are, and know how their own efforts support the key tasks of the team as a whole. In terms of morale, what are these key tasks?

The Leader's Key Tasks

There are three areas in which every team leader must excel:

- communicating the challenge
- setting the example, and
- communicating confidence

The Challenge The first requirement of a leader is that people will follow. This can best be ensured by the provision of a vision in the form of a statement of the future with which people can identify.

Challenging targets, set in a climate of confidence, create self-esteem and a sense of 'we can do it' in the team. Emphasis on the challenging aspects of targets arouses the basic motivating drives in people for achievement. This is vital for high morale. The team members must know that the team is engaged in the real stuff of life and that their existence as such has real meaning. The challenge need not be the challenge of an Everest or an Apollo moon shot; it need only be the challenge of some task not tackled previously. For the leader, the key task is not only to help the team set challenging targets, but to keep the team reminded of the significance of its work. When the team works well, he should say so — loudly and clearly — not only to the team, but to those around. This sense of significance helps to keep the team's morale high. As one commentator puts it:

> Leaders have a significant role in creating the state of mind that is the society. They can serve as symbols of the moral unity of the society. They can express the values that hold society together. Most important, they can conceive and articulate goals that lift people out of their petty preoccupations, carry them above the conflicts that tear a society apart, and unite them in pursuit of objectives worthy of their best efforts.[2]

This, then, is the first key task for the leader.

The Example The second key task is setting the example. The leader needs to behave in the manner in which he wants the team members to behave. Leaders need to project an image of competence, success and unity. Emphasis on the example and the unity arouses in people the need for affiliation.

Philip Greenslade finishes his book on leadership with a chapter entitled 'Starter for 10'. In it he emphasises the importance of setting an example. He says, talking to leaders: 'Be ready to change yourself. Change begins with us . . . When I show genuine emotion, others know that I am not a plastic man, unaffected by the need for change urged on them.'[3]

Not only must the leader be an example of commitment, but

also of care for and sensitivity to others. Jesus called his team
with the words, 'follow me'[4] and St Paul echoed these words as
he encouraged a new team — 'You became imitators of us'.[5]
What kind of example are you to your team? Can they look to
you for the right attitudes and behaviour? Can you say, 'Do as I
do'?

If you set the challenge, if you set the example, then you are
more than half-way to having a team that works well. But there
is one more key task for the leader.

Communicating Confidence Confidence breeds confidence. A
strong conviction of the rightness of the team's mission and
actions is necessary for confidence. The more confident the
leader appears to be to his team, the higher the standards the
team will accept in task terms.

> Positive self-regard seems to exert its force by creating in
> others a sense of confidence and high expectation, not very
> different from the fabled Pygmalion effect. When Ian
> McGregor took over the chairmanship of the British Steel
> Corporation, his first order of business was to restore the
> morale of middle management. He couldn't offer his
> executives the financial rewards customary in money-
> making companies, but he could provide motivation by
> building up their independence and confidence.[6]

When the team leader fulfils in the areas of challenge,
example and confidence, the team responds with high
performance, emulation and trust. The result is a team with
high morale. Let us look now at what these actions and attitudes
in the leader will mean for the team.

Members' Key Tasks

The team leader should sit down once a year with each member of his team to set down his areas of key results. Each
member should be encouraged to think about his role and tasks
and — in discussion with his leader — come to understand how
his role fits into the team, and to recognise the results his role
exists to produce. He must be clear about his authority and the
resources and services he can control or call upon.

High performance Given a high challenge from the leader and a
growing sense of confidence, the team member is able to respond with high-quality contributions. These might be in the
volume and standard of work, or in the value of his contribution
to team discussions. Let me give an example. I was once asked

to help set up a small manufacturing plant in a rural area. The main plant was 30 miles away in a large population centre. My responsibility was for the training of staff, and the target was to raise production levels to within 20% of the main plant in 6 months. Managers at the main plant argued that rural workers could not be trained to the same level as those used to operating in factories! You can imagine my approach – I simply shared this view with the staff! I was also careful to stress my own belief that they could not only match the production levels, but could exceed them. Within 4 months, production levels were 20% above those of the main plant and the number of rejects was 15% lower! These people had responded to a challenge. This is what happens when a team works well.

Emulation In setting an example for the team, the leader is modelling the behaviour he believes will lead to success. His enthusiasm leads to their enthusiasm. His vision becomes their vision. His standards become their standards. His priorities become their priorities. The key task for the team member is to follow. The young person who has a hero seeks to act like him, dress like him and talk like him. The toy cupboards in my home are full of the relics of past heroes – from the Wild West through Star Trek to Star Wars and most of the world's great battle-fields! Depending on when you visit us, you run the risk of being scalped, 'beamed-up', mown down or bombarded with 90 decibels of Michael Jackson! – on high performance days, perhaps even all four!

Make a list of five things you do that you would like other members of the team to copy:

1 _____

2 _____

3 _____

4 _____

5 _____

Belief and Trust The third key activity for the team member is of a different character altogether. Belief in self, and trust in others are among the more important *inner* experiences which come from being in a team that is working well. This world sends us many opportunities to fail and to lose faith in ourselves. The strong team provides an environment not only in which the hurts of living can be healed, but also in which the confidence in self can be restored.

If the leader can enhance the self-regard of the members and can encourage them to view the future positively rather than fearfully, then the team will work well and morale will be high.

We have discussed the leader's key tasks and the members' key tasks. We can now illustrate these in the following diagram.

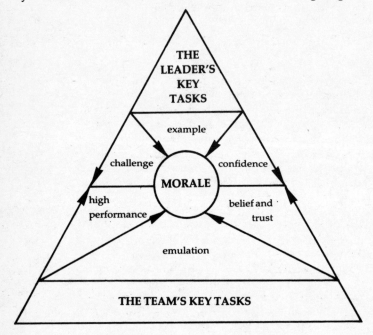

The Team That Works Well

Review

After an agreed period, or at regular points in the year, the team member should discuss with his leader the key tasks he has achieved. If this analysis is objective and unemotional, it should help to identify:

- future objectives and key tasks
- further necessary changes in the team's resources, services, and authority
- the potential of the member for greater responsibility
- training needed by the member
- personal failure on the part of either the member or his leader or anybody else, and possible reasons for it, and plans to avoid repetition.

Chapters 11, 12 and 13 provide alternative and more detailed methods of reviewing performance.

Let us check how well your team is working. Place a circle around the number that best fits your team's situation.

1 My team is engaged in tasks which are
challenging   5
routine   4
tedious   3
confused   2

2 The leadership in my team is
outstanding   5
mediocre   4
poor   3
non-existent   2

3 My leader makes me feel
strong   5
accepted   4
inadequate   3
a failure   2

4 On the whole, my team's performance is
outstanding   5
acceptable   4
mixed   3
poor   2

5 I can look at my leader as an example
always   5
often   4
sometimes   3
never   2

6 Looking around the team I feel
pleasure   5
disappointed   4
frustrated   3
embarrassed   2

If you have scored less than 24, then your team is not working as well as it should. What will you do to improve the morale of the team?

PART 4
Evaluating Your Performance

...AND WHEN IT DOESN'T

Chapter 10

Not every team can be successful all the time. Unfortunately, many teams are not successful most of the time!

> The firemen's strike in the UK in 1978 made possible one of the great animal rescue attempts of all time. Valiantly, the British Army had taken over emergency fire-fighting and on 14th January they were called out by an elderly lady in South London to retrieve her cat which had become trapped up a tree. They arrived with impressive haste and soon discharged their duty. So grateful was the lady that she invited them all in for tea. Driving off later, with fond farewells completed, they ran over the cat.[1]

Improving Your Performance

As we begin the fourth section of this book, we should remember that if building an effective team is a difficult task at the best of times, it is almost impossible at the worst of times. When the team does not work well, we should not redouble our efforts; we should stop and take a good hard look at the problem. *What* is going wrong? *When* is it going wrong? *Why* is it going wrong? To hide from the problems, to deny their existence, to move ahead as though nothing was amiss – these are the strategies of weakness and failure. Yet I see them all around: in governments that turn blind eyes to social problems; in boardrooms where growing competition is ignored; in churches whose pews are emptying; in families whose relationships are deteriorating. It is true that at first glance, and even at second and third glances, solutions are not easy to find; but easy solutions do not necessarily challenge and they often address the symptoms rather than the sources of the problem.

Some time ago I was asked to evaluate the performance of a manufacturing company. It had been a good year financially, but the managing director was not happy; 'I want my team to be more concerned with tomorrow's opportunities than yesterday's failures,' he explained. 'They are too cautious, too fearful, and that is reducing their ability to be creative and innovative.' When I asked how he knew that things were wrong, he replied, 'I don't know, Dave, I just feel it. That's why I want you to evaluate our performance.' So I developed a way of providing him with the information he needed to make decisions. I constructed a questionnaire which was then sent to 100 members of staff. The results showed that his feelings were correct – but not in all parts of the company. Some departments were indeed looking to the future. By learning from the successes of others, those teams which had not been working well were able to adopt some of the more successful practices.

In this section, I will give you a number of ideas to help you improve your performance.

Why Teams Fail

Not all of the ideas and insights we have discussed in *Team Spirit* are applicable to your team, but many of them are – since all are insights about people working with people. Successful teams are alike in their success, but as Tolstoy observed: 'All happy families resemble each other, while each unhappy family is unhappy in its own way.'[2]

Let us look back over the way we have come, for in each chapter we have considered the essential elements of a successful team. Why do teams fail? Here are some of the main reasons.

No Concepts

Each team leader must have in his mind an ideal model of what his team should be. Such an ideal should be his vision for his team. Whether you take your model from history or the present day seems to matter little, but if you have no vision, then you are a blind leader in the dark. It is, however, unlikely that all your team members are equally visionless – one or two know what should be done, and unfortunately, their frustrations will create stress in themselves and tension in the group.

Wrong Style

Teams need different types of leadership during their existence. There are times when strong, directive leadership is required, particularly in times of crisis and threat. Decisions need to be taken quickly, action implemented without hesitation or question – but these times are rare. A team which lives in a constant state of crisis soon exhausts itself. Teams are interdependent groups of people and malfunction if dominated by the leader or one or two members. The goal-keeper who saves 100 shots in the course of a football match may be doing a great job, but he certainly isn't part of a great team!

Wrong Expectations

What do you expect from your team and its leadership? I remember working with a team that had recently recruited two new members. They had been selected because of their standing in the local community, but they thought they had been invited because of their ideas, enthusiasm and ability to get things done. The team was soon in total disarray. The newcomers were seen as belittling all that had gone before, while the older members were viewed as impeding progress. By the time I was called in, the confusion was complete. No one could understand anyone else; stereotypes had been formed, and the group was about to self-destruct! My approach was to ask each member to take time to write down what he or she expected from the group and what their hopes for the future were. These were then transferred to sheets of flip chart paper. Lo and behold, the team found common ground! Not only common ground, but common concerns, too.

If you find members of your team taking up positions you cannot understand, then check your expectations. Write them down, then share them with the leader and other members.

Low Commitment

There are few more difficult problems to cope with than low commitment in a team. Without commitment –

- decisions will not be followed through
- quality and quantity of work will be low
- there will be no common vision
- there will be little satisfaction and
- relationships will deteriorate.

The scope for remedial action is limited, but depending on the source of the problem, the following approaches might work:

1 Revitalise the team with a change of membership.
2 Create a new vision for the team by talking about what you will be doing in five years' time.
3 Give positive feed-back, and reward any actions you value and want to see repeated.
4 Increase involvement in the team. If the team is being carried by one or two members, begin to share the load by asking for help.
5 Change the roles around.
6 Talk to each member individually about your concerns for the future and what he or she believes needs to be done.
7 If you can do nothing else, commit yourself to one year of setting an example of a committed team member. If nothing changes, then withdraw from the team and put your own commitment to more profitable work.

Poor Skills

Your team may be at the bottom of the fourth division because that is where it belongs! To change this, a systematic pro-gramme of skill development will make all the difference. In one company for which I was consultant, my role was to act as personal coach to the managing director's team. I attended the monthly management meeting, then spent time with all the team members, helping them to review their contributions and develop ways to improve their work during the next month.

Developing team skills takes time, so do not be disappointed if progress is slow. Recognise, also, that some people cannot make much improvement in their performance – they will always be fourth division players or, worse, fourth division spectators! It may be that the best approach to these people is to remove them from the team and invite them on those occasions when their specialism will be of some value.

Inappropriate Structures

This is often a difficult problem to spot since it will give rise to such varied symptoms as:

- overworked members
- bad communication
- confused roles
- conflict
- duplication of effort, etc.

The easiest way to check whether your structure is correct or not is to go back to the purpose of the team. Ask yourself:

1 What is the team set up to do?
2 What are its main activities?
3 How do these activities relate to each other?
4 What would be happening if the team was really working well?
5 What is wrong now?
6 How could we re-structure to get from 5 to 4!?

Remember that a change in structure will result in an extended period of uncertainty, so often it is easier to ask:
7 What should we be doing more of and less of?
This last question will help you make better use of your current structure.

No Growth

You only have one life, so you cannot afford to spend any of it in situations which do not let you grow: socially, spiritually or intellectually. Growth is inhibited in groups as a result of:

- repressive leadership
- no vision
- no challenge
- high task orientation in the group with low concern for individual needs.

If you find yourself in a static team, you must share your

concerns with the leader. First, be clear about what it is you wish to achieve. It may be the opportunity to use your gifts to a greater degree. It may be the chance to take on new responsibilities or learn new skills. It may be to have a clearer sense of direction or to have more satisfaction from your team membership. Write it down as a personal target, then take it to the team leader for discussion. Consider how you are going to influence her and also what you will do if she does not listen to you. A limited amount of alternatives are open to you:

- accept her repression and put up with it
- say that you will raise the matter with the team at its next meeting
- say that you will raise the matter with the next level of 'management'
- wait for a better opportunity to negotiate
- use the ultimate sanction and leave the group.

Do not try to undermine the position of the leader or stage a revolution. Your own needs for growth, although important, should not be met at the expense of others.

Poor Procedures

This common problem is more easily dealt with. Chapter 8 on team meetings contains much that will improve the way the team operates. An approach usually acceptable is to adopt a meeting review form, such as the one opposite. It should be used initially at three consecutive meetings of the group. At the end of the meeting, each member should complete the assessment checklist and share one of the areas for improvement. Agreement should be made on which area the team will try to improve at the next meeting. This should be recorded. You will find that just reading through the list of 15 aspects actually results in improvements!

Lack of Discipline

There are four common manifestations of poor discipline in teams:

- people talking at once
- interrupting speakers

TEAMWORK ASSESSMENT CHECKLIST

Aspect of Teamwork	Assessment		
	Deficient	Adequate	Strong
1 Gathering information			
2 Setting goals			
3 Planning			
4 Managing time in the meeting			
5 Creating ideas			
6 Evaluating			
7 Deciding			
8 Getting into action			
9 Reviewing			
10 All members contributing			
11 Open interaction			
12 Agenda setting			
13 Task orientation			
14 Group orientation			
15 Individual orientation			

Three areas where my team needs to improve are:

A _____

B _____

C _____

156

       − time overruns/late starts

    − failure to follow through decisions.

Much can be done by a good leader or chairperson, but there is nothing to beat self-discipline!

Feed-back is one of the most powerful ways to influence meeting disciplines − simply tell the group what is happening, for example:

1 'Sorry, John, I missed what you were saying; I find it hard to concentrate when more than one person is talking.'
   or
2 'I would like to hear what John was going to say. I don't think he had finished when Bill gave us that useful thought.'
   or
3 'I am getting worried about the time we're spending on this item. Where will we make it up, or will we drop an item or two from tonight's agenda?'
   or
4 'My understanding was that we had agreed to leave this point to another meeting and now we have started discussing it again. Can I just check what it is we are going to do?'

(There are some further guide-lines for giving feed-back in Chapter 12.)

Low Creativity

A group which is short on ideas and long on tradition may find itself faced with a number of problems, long-standing in nature. This may be due to the fact that between them, the group members are unable to come up with any fresh approaches to the problem.

Low creativity can be caused by a number of factors:

1 Insufficient time given to thinking as a group or individually. If the problem to be solved is difficult or important, you need at least two hours just to generate and explore ideas. Creativity cannot be rushed and can rarely be produced on demand.
2 An overly critical climate in the team. Creativity needs a supportive climate. Individuals will be cautious if they expect to be criticised for suggesting 'way-out' ideas. However, it is often true that the 'way-out' suggestion can lead to a very useful idea.
3 Strict routines and a stiff atmosphere will restrict creativity. A problem-solving meeting should be less formal.
4 Incorrect procedures. The thinking process is helped by vis-

ual recording on flip charts or blackboard. Each idea should be written up on the board.
5 Premature evaluation of ideas. The ideas should be gathered before they are evaluated. List all the suggestions and only then go back and evaluate them, ranking each idea A, B or C − A being 'very useful', B being 'possible', and C being 'not useful'. The A's can then be ranked according to how close they come to meeting the team's objectives.

No Challenge

Strong teams have a strong sense of identity − the members belong together and feel right about belonging to this team. In this state of high association, the team is nevertheless at risk from a number of traps:

− that no one will be prepared to question or challenge the way the group operates

− that the need for agreement and harmony will override the need for challenge

− that the group will continue to pursue outdated targets

− that disagreement is seen as rebellion, or worse, as treachery.

I recall a classic example of how easy it is for a group to fall into these traps. It was August and the place was a small cove in Spain, just across the French border. The Mediterranean sparkled in the early morning sun as we ate our breakfast on the beach. Another fine day was promised − swimming, sailing and relaxing in the shadows of the towering cliffs. We were eight − two families on holiday together and really enjoying the experience of being with close friends in a holiday environment. It was the beginning of our second week. Idyllic.

'Who fancies a trip to Andorra?' John asked. I thought, 'Andorra is over 100 miles away, and we only have one car. It will be murder with four children and four adults in this heat!' but instead of saying what I thought, I replied, 'It should be a nice trip up into the mountains.' My wife added, 'And there are supposed to be good duty-free bargains in Andorra. Yes, let's go, but what about the children, perhaps they would prefer to stay on the beach.' A chorus of 'No's' and 'I want to come too's' ended the discussion. So we gathered up our beach gear and piled into the car. Although the Datsun 2500 series is roomy, it's not quite roomy enough for 8, hence the reason why we had come down through France by motor-rail. Nevertheless, we did all fit − just!

The road from the Mediterranean coast up to Andorra is spectacular. In the cool of the morning the air was punctuated with 'ooh's' and 'aah's' and 'Look at that!' But by mid-morning more than the engine was overheating!

Andorra was hot, crowded and a long, long way from the cool of our cliff-shaded beach. By the time we returned to our villa, no one had the energy left to complain – recriminations had to wait till breakfast, served for those who were not quite ill enough to stay in bed!

'Well, at least we got some duty free,' ventured my wife, breaking the stony silence. 'We could have got that at Boulogne instead of paying nearly £30.00 on petrol,' I countered. 'But you wanted to see the mountains,' she pointed out. 'Me? Not me! I wanted to stay on the beach. It was John who wanted to go. I just didn't want to split up the party.' John rose, 'Look, I thought you were getting bored on the beach all day – all I wanted was to make sure that you really enjoyed the day. If you had wanted to stay on the beach, you should have said so!'

He was right, of course. There we were, 4 adults and 4 children doing what we wanted to do and suddenly, faced with an alternative which no one wanted, we all put our better judgement on hold and travelled over 300 miles in an overcrowded mobile oven!

We had become victims of the 'unity syndrome' in which a team of close-knit members take action in opposition to what they really want to do and therefore defeat the very purpose they are trying to achieve. The unity syndrome has its origin in *agreement!* The team is so strong that when it needs to disagree it cannot. Many teams and many countries have taken side trips or occasionally, terminal trips down routes they did not want to travel. For us, on our holiday in Spain, it was only one bad day, but unless your team learns to manage disagreement *and* agreement, it may find itself embarking on a journey from which it will never return.[3]

No one is helped if you keep your doubts or concerns to yourself. The great American Space Shuttle disaster of 1986 happened despite the fact that many of the engineers had profound reservations about aspects of the design and of the programme. Silence is not loyalty and can be fatal.

Summary

For many of us in poorly performing teams, our only source of comfort is that they do not meet very often! We can grit our teeth, grin and bear it for a couple of hours a month, and if it gets bad, we can always take it out on the cat!

I have stressed that although it is a delight to work in an effective team, it is also hard work to make it effective and to keep it effective. Perhaps the effort for you is not worth the bother — ie your commitment is low because of the limited return.

In the following two chapters, I will deal with the topic of assessment and evaluation. These are difficult concepts to apply — easy to understand. In industry, in the voluntary sectors of our society, in education, in commerce and in our private lives, we shy away from evaluating and judging people and situations; it is easier to pass by on the other side or ignore the problems and inadequacies and hope they will go away, than to face up to them and try to overcome them.

If you would rather not be bothered with the trouble of trying to change yourself and helping others to change, then I suggest that you move directly to Chapter 14. If, on the other hand, your commitment is such that you are prepared to put yourself at risk for the sake of others, then read on. The choice is yours. For those about to move to Chapter 14, you should first of all return to Chapter 1 and the questionnaire on page 22. You may wish to change some of your answers!

EVALUATING THE TEAM: CHECKLISTS

Chapter 11

To make the most of your team will require effort on your part, whether you are the leader or a member.

As we have seen, a team needs targets if it is to work effectively, and the team must support these targets. But simply setting targets and getting support for them is no guarantee of success. The team must work towards these targets. Sometimes the team will make progress; at other times it will encounter setbacks, but at all times the team should remain aware of how it is doing and be prepared to evaluate its progress.

Evaluating Performance

The team leader and the members need to be aware of what is happening in the team at all times. The leader should evaluate regularly:

- his or her own performance
- the performance of the group as a whole
- the performance of individual members and
- the conduct of meetings and other activities of the team.

These evaluations can be done informally, but it is more helpful to approach the evaluation of performance in a structured way. This ensures that fewer areas are overlooked and also that the evaluations are consistent over time and from member to member.

In this chapter is presented a number of checklists that teams might usefully include in their activities. These are designed to:

- check performance
- provide data for planning
- provide ideas for improvement
- provide suggestions for training
- provide feed-back to the leader and the members on their performance.

A Framework for Evaluation

Whether you are evaluating a large organisation, a small team or an individual, there are certain steps that need to be followed. The diagram below shows a six-step framework for evaluation:

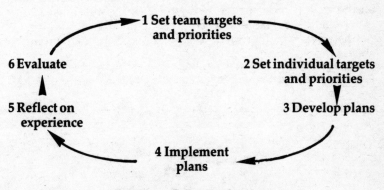

Framework For Evaluation

I have dealt with these six steps at various points in this book, but now I want to concentrate on evaluation. It is the most difficult part of the cycle.

There are two major approaches to evaluation, the first is by use of check-lists, the second is by discussion. In this chapter I will deal with evaluation by checklist and in Chapter 12 I will examine the interview/discussion approach. The evaluation sheets in this chapter are not meant to be used as means of 'punishing' group members or the group leader. So it is important to establish ground rules for their use. Here are some useful guidelines.

1 Say only unto others what you would have them say to you.
2 All responses are to be confidential within the team.
3 No action arising from the responses is to be forced on any member. All action is to be by agreement.
4 No negative feed-back to be given without a corresponding piece of positive feed-back; ie unless you can say something positive, you are not allowed to say anything negative!
5 No feed-back to be given unless you are prepared to help the person improve.

Additional guidelines are given in Chapter 13, page 181-182.

How Is Your Own Membership?

How do you rate as a team member? The first checklist is designed for you to check your own performance as a team member. The form helps you think about your behaviour in groups, meetings and committees. First, read over the scales and, on each one, put a cross indicating the place on the scale that describes your typical behaviour in groups. After marking all the scales, pick out the two which you would most like to change and set a target in each area. Some activities which are not listed may be important to you, so write these down in the spaces provided.

Checklist for Your Own Performance

COMMUNICATION SKILLS	Need to do more		Satisfactory			Need to do less	
1 Talking in the team							
	1	2	3	4	5	6	7
2 Being brief and concise							
3 Being assertive							
4 Involving others							
5 Listening actively							
6 Thinking before I talk							
7 Keeping my remarks on the topic							
8							
9							

164

OBSERVATION SKILLS	Need to do more		Satisfactory			Need to do less	
1 Noting tension in the group							
	1	2	3	4	5	6	7
2 Noting who talks to whom							
3 Noting interest levels in the group							
4 Sensing the feelings of individual members							
5 Noting who is being 'left out' or dominated							
6 Noting reactions							
7 Noting when the group avoids a topic							
8							
9							

PROBLEM-SOLVING SKILLS	Need to do more		Satisfactory			Need to do less	
1 Stating problems or targets							
	1	2	3	4	5	6	7
2 Asking for ideas or opinions							
3 Giving ideas							
4 Evaluating ideas							
5 Summarising discussion							
6 Clarifying issues							
7 Decision making							
8 Pushing for action							
9 Reviewing performance							

MORALE-BUILDING SKILLS	Need to do more		Satisfactory			Need to do less	
1 Encouraging challenging targets							
	1	2	3	4	5	6	7
2 Using the full talent of the group							
3 Helping people reach agreement							
4 Building confidence							
5 Maintaining the value of individuals in face of group pressure or failure							
6							
7							

SOCIAL RELATIONSHIPS	Need to do more		Satisfactory			Need to do less	
1 Competing with others							
	1	2	3	4	5	6	7
2 Acting dominant towards others							
3 Relying on others							
4 Being helpful							
5 Being protective							
6 Calling attention to myself and my needs							
7 Being able to stand up for my own targets							
8							

GENERAL	Need to do more		Satisfactory			Need to do less	
1 Understand- ing why I do what I do							
	1	2	3	4	5	6	7
2 Encouraging comments on my own behaviour							
3 Accepting help willingly							
4 Making my mind up firmly							
5 Criticising myself							
6 Being patient							
7 Taking time to think							
8							
9							

The two areas in which I want to see some change are:

1 _____

2 _____

The target I will set myself in each area is:

1 _____

2 _____

Do not begin to assess other people until you have assessed yourself. As a member of the team, the road to improvement begins at your own door.

Evaluating the Teamwork

All groups must face and solve a number of problems to work together effectively. We have considered many of them in the course of this text. Let us now focus on some key problems.

Consider the eight areas of teamwork described below and select two areas where the effectiveness of the group is high. Then select two areas where the effectiveness of the group is low. Mark the TWO contributing areas with '+', and the TWO detracting areas with '−'.

1 *Setting objectives and targets* − How well does the team reconcile different individual targets and ensure that group targets are clear and agreed upon? How well does the team ensure that targets are practical and criteria for review are understood?

2 *Structure and procedure* − How well does the team explore the different members' preferences for structured or unstructured discussion, and to what extent is it necessary to adhere to a definite procedure?

3 *Doing and feeling* − How well does the team balance the need of some members concerned primarily to get the job done, and the need of others who think that the feelings of members are more important − so that both feel at ease?

4 *Decisions and concensus* − How clear is the decision-making process? Do the members ensure that there is sufficient commitment to decisions, and that the decisions are properly carried out?

5 *Authority and dependency* — How well does the team deal with members who have different preferences for independence, dependence, or inter-dependence?

6 *Membership and involvement* — How does the group deal with different feelings about being involved as active members of the group and the varying feelings about the amount of participation by themselves and others?

7 *Giving and receiving feed-back* — How well do members help each other by commenting on the contributions they find most useful or unuseful? Do they help each other learn from experience?

8 *Communications* — Is the level of trust and openness in the group sufficient to allow good communications without members feeling too exposed or defensive?

It is not suggested that these eight areas are distinct and unrelated, so you may find it useful to consider whether there is a pattern to your team's areas of strength and weakness.

The Members' Evaluation of the Teamwork

A leader needs feed-back on the team's performance and on his or her performance as a leader. The checklist opposite helps the leader to understand how the team is viewed by its members. Place a tick in the column which best applies to your group. It should be completed by the whole team.

It would be helpful to share the results of this checklist with the team and consider how the situation might be improved. Be careful to tackle a limited number of areas for improvement, not more than three.

The Team Evaluates the Leadership

It might take some time for you to feel strong enough to use the checklist on page 172 in your team, yet there are few better ways to improve your performance than to ask for comments from your team. Here are some questions about the team leader. Please indicate which of the following phrases apply to the team leader by placing a tick in the appropriate box.

No	SOURCES OF DISSATISFACTION	Does Not Apply in This Team	Applies in This Team	Strongly Applies in This Team
1	Lack of clearly defined team targets			
2	Insufficient responsibility and authority given to team members			
3	Gifts not recognised			
4	Heavy work load for some members			
5	Inadequate training for tasks			
6	Excessive rules and regulations			
7	Too many crises			
8	Poor communications with other teams			
9	Uncertainty about the future			
10	Unco-operative attitudes			
11	Excessive interference by other members in my tasks			
12	Too much paperwork			
13	Lack of recognition for effort			
14	Excessive 'political' manoeuvring			
15	Too many meetings			
16	Meetings too long			
17	Too many changes in plans			
18	Shortage of resources			
19	Too many changes in team membership			
20	(other)			
21	(other)			

No.	YOUR GROUP LEADER	Always	Mostly	Some-times	Seldom	Never
1	Allows team members to do things the way they think best					
2	Is decisive					
3	Is prepared to take reasonable risks					
4	Expects directions and instructions to be followed to the letter					
5	Decides in detail what team members should do					
6	Is prepared to try out other people's ideas					
7	Plans the work well					
8	Interferes with the work of team members					
9	Ensures that people know what is expected of them					
10	Is helpful when we have a problem					
11	Keeps us informed about policies and plans					
12	Is prepared to change opinion					
13	Is fair to everybody					
14	Talks things over with us before making changes					
15	Other significant feature					
16	Other significant feature					

Once again, the team should work to improve performance on a narrow front — focus on one or two behaviours the team wishes the leader to change, rather than trying to introduce changes in all areas.

The Team Evaluates Its Meetings

The transforming of experience into learning comes with review, so at the end of each team meeting the group should review its performance. The checklist here will help and may be used in conjunction with the Teamwork Assessment on page 155.

Meeting Review

1 Was the meeting well run?   YES/NO

2 How much real progress do you think the meeting made?

None   Great
at all _____ progress
      0   1   2   3   4   5   6   7

3 Did the team maintain its unity or did it tend to be split by division?

Experienced   Maintained
division _____ unity
      0   1   2   3   4   5   6   7

4 Was the meeting clear about its targets or was there some confusion?

Confused   Clear
targets _____ targets
      0   1   2   3   4   5   6   7

5 Did all members of the meeting participate fully, or was the meeting dominated by one or a few individuals?

Dominated   Partici-
_____ pative
      0   1   2   3   4   5   6   7

6 How much digression from the agenda of the meeting took place?

Considerable   No
digression _____ digression
      0   1   2   3   4   5   6   7

7 State one action *you* could take next time the team meets
which would improve performance.

_____

_____

_____

_____

It is helpful if the team shares its responses to this questionnaire, particularly item 7. Some teams actually find it useful to
record the responses to 7 in the minutes.

Evaluation Can Be Fun
I was trained in group dynamics in the late 1960s at a time
when the philosophy seemed to be: 'If it's painful, it must be
good for you!' Many of the group experiences used by my tutors
then were designed for maximum impact and — so it seemed —
maximum hurt. I am glad to say that the world of training has
learned a lot since those days. Learning can be fun. Developing
your team can be enjoyable, provided you are prepared to
recognise your need to learn and can laugh at your mistakes.

EVALUATING THE TEAM: INTERVIEWS

Chapter 12

Why Evaluate?

Why should you evaluate team members individually? Is it not good enough simply to evaluate the team as a whole? There are a number of advantages to both the leader and the member if you focus on both the team and the members. In my experience, it is often the members who wish the evaluation to take place, rather than the leader. The reasons for this are plain when you consider that evaluations recognise and document the team member's performance. They also give the team member an opportunity to discuss his feelings about his role in the team, his work, his performance, and the leadership. Such a discussion provides the team member with support for and information on his personal development and training needs, as well as identifying targets for the coming year. In addition, evaluations may determine the team member's future direction, for example into leadership of his own team.

Thus personal evaluation is a wholly *positive* activity aimed at reviewing and improving the team member's performance. It is not, however, an activity to be entered into lightly. In this chapter I will deal in some depth with this crucial, performance-improving tool.

What Is Needed?

The term 'evaluation' is objectionable in some circles, and so a number of other words have been adopted. These include 'appraisal', 'assessment', 'review' and 'performance discussion'. Use whatever term is acceptable. Look again at the Framework for Evaluation on page 161. This gives a number of clues as to what is required for effective evaluation.

First, the team needs to be clear about its own purposes, targets and priorities. It is impossible for the soldier to be an effective fighting unit if he does not know which way the battle is moving. Second, the team member should have a written guide to or description of his role in the team. Evaluation cannot be conducted without some kind of a yard-stick. Third, each member should have written down his or her personal targets. At the first evaluation, these will probably not exist. But at the end of the evaluation, targets will be agreed, and these can then form a basis of the next evaluation. Fourth, the evaluation should be open and yet confidential. Any records kept should be seen by the member − no secret files, please! Fifth, the effective evaluation needs to be backed by training and development.

Now it may be that your team does not have all, or any of the above. Well, don't be downcast: you have to start somewhere. Start by asking for an evaluation discussion.

Preparing for Evaluation

Do not spring an evaluation session on someone. Give at least four weeks' notice. None of this, 'I was just passing, so I thought I'd take the time to pop in to evaluate your performance!' Preparation is important. Both the leader and the member should make notes beforehand. It is useful to use some form to collect the thoughts of the participants. The following example illustrates what can be usefully thought about before the event:

Preparation Form

CONFIDENTIAL

from _____

to _____

Date of Evaluation discussion _____

PREPARATION FOR THE EVALUATION DISCUSSION

In connection with your membership of the _____ Team/Committee, and as part of our commitment to improve your development and use of gifts and skills, I should like to discuss with you and to hear your views on your performance during the past year, your work plan for the next year, and how your potential may be developed to the full.

To help us both obtain benefit from the discussion, a short list of questions is attached. Answering these in advance should enable us to clarify our thoughts in preparation for our talk, and to note any particular points we feel we should discuss in depth.

You are free to use this form as you wish. You may keep it yourself, but let me have a copy before the interview, or bring it with you for reference. It is your own property and does not have to be attached to the evaluation form unless you especially want it to be. A summary of our discussion and conclusions will be recorded on the appraisal form, a copy of which will be given to you for your own records.

1 *Present Contribution to the Team*

    (a)   Set down in order of importance a brief list of what you consider to have been your main tasks and contributions to the team during the past year.

    (b)   Which of your skills showed themselves most clearly in the team during the last year? How could these strengths be exploited?

    (c)   What have you done least well? How could these weaknesses be overcome?

2 **Future Contribution to the Team**

   (a) Were there any obstacles which hindered you from achieving what you intended? Are they likely to recur? If so, how could they be eliminated?

   (b) If you were team leader, what changes would you make in the way your talents and gifts are used?

   (c) What action can you take to improve your contribution to the team?

   (d) What additional things might the team do to help you improve your value to the team?

3   *Work Plans*
    (a)   What do you think should be the main targets in your work for the team in the next year?

    (b)   What standards do you think we should use to assess your performance during the coming year?

4   *Development*
    (a)   Do you think that you need more training or experience to enable you to function better in the team? If so, of what kind?

    (b)   What do you hope to be doing in (say) three years' time within the organisation/church? Is there any training that you feel you need to prepare you for the future?

5   *Other Points*
Are there any other issues you wish to raise in relation to your work in the team?

Beginning an Evaluation

Many people experience quite a high level of stress before an evaluation. They worry about what will be said; will they be criticised? How will they cope? How will they say what they want to say? So it is important to take time to establish a rapport. An evaluation session should take at least 1 hour, but not more than 2, so you should take about 10 minutes to help create the right atmosphere. Have a cup of tea and talk about how you're feeling — a bit nervous, excited, anticipatory, etc. Ask the member how he or she feels.   Be ready and welcoming, even if you have some hard things to say — you are going to say them because it is in the best interest of yourself, the member and the team. So act to show that the individual and the event are both important. Sit side by side, not face to face, and certainly not across a desk. Think about your non-verbal messages!

Getting the Facts

Remember that this is the member's meeting; it is for his benefit primarily, so you must be prepared to listen. Ask questions and let the team member talk. Do not interrupt; if necessary, make a few notes of issue you want to explore further.

If you disagree with the views being expressed, do not challenge at this point; instead seek to understand the member's position. Exercise that skill of empathy. Get into his shoes; learn what it feels like to be sitting there with that opinion. Be open-minded. You do not have and will never have *all* the facts, and you will have even fewer of the feelings. So avoid taking up a rigid position. Be prepared to change your view if you get new information.

Once the member has run through the details on his preparation form and any other items, then it is your turn to state clearly how you have seen the member's performance since the last session. Stress the positive features; be clear and direct about those aspects of performance which were not up to standard, and finish on a positive note.

Give the member plenty of opportunity to discuss and question your views, then summarise and record the facts as they have been agreed.

Tackling the Problems

From the opening discussions, a number of problems will surface. How should these be dealt with?

1   List them. Write them on paper or on a flip chart where both of you can see them. Agree on the list.
2   Decide which are the priorities for examination in this meeting — probably not more than three.
3   Take each one in turn and focus on the future. This is not a trial! Discuss what can be done to ensure that the problem does not arise again or is tackled in a different way.
4   Focus on action, not attitudes! Decide what should be done and the standards to be achieved. Do not, for example, say 'I want your attitude to Don to improve' rather say, 'I want you to let Don finish what he has to say in the team meetings.'
5   Only accept win/win actions. These are actions in which everyone gains, the team, the leader and the member.

When you have agreed on the actions, move on to planning.

Planning to Improve

Many ideas for improvement stay as ideas because no attention is given to planning. Each action should be described as a target and it is helpful to use some form of planning chart. The one below is taken from my book on time management, *Seconds Away!*.[1] Begin by filling in the target, column 7; then work through from 1 to 6. One sheet should be completed for each main target.

Documentation

Make your notes immediately after the interview. This will ensure that you do not forget any important aspects. There are a number of approaches to keeping records. The most common is to make a few long-hand notes; however it is probably easier and more consistent to use a form.

There are two main types of forms. The first (labelled I, p 184) gives the team leader more scope to express his own views and opinions, since it asks a number of questions. The second (labelled II, p 185) is much longer and more structured. It asks for many of the responses to be on a fixed scale. The latter approach is easier to handle in very large teams and organisations. Whatever way you document it, the notes should be shown to the team member concerned.

(1) My Present Situation	(2) My Strengths	(3) My Weaknesses	(4) My Next Possible Steps	(5) The Time Required	(6) Review Date and Method	(7) My Target

An Organic Planning Chart

I Performance Evaluation
(To Be Completed by the Team Leader)

1   What were the key areas and targets set for the past year?

_____

_____

2   How well did the member perform in these areas?

_____

_____

3   Were there any key factors which particularly contributed to the member's success or failure in those areas?

_____

_____

_____

4   What areas are important for the coming year, and what targets have been agreed with the member?

_____

_____

_____

5   What training has the member received in the past year?

_____

_____

_____

6   In the light of the evaluation discussion, what training do you suggest for the coming year?

_____

_____

_____

7   What additional support is needed?

_____

_____

_____

This document was seen by and discussed with the team member on
Date...

II Performance Evaluation
(To Be Completed by the Team Leader)

Name _____

Position in team _____

Section A

1 KNOWLEDGE — of function, operations and area of activity — keeps up with current developments in his area — knowledge of team policies and procedures.

1	2	3	4	5
Poor	Fair	Good	Very Good	Excellent

2 PERFORMANCE — quality of work — accuracy of instructions, statements — productiveness —interest — enthusiasm — industry

1	2	3	4	5
Poor	Fair	Good	Very Good	Excellent

3 RESOURCEFULNESS — initiative — vision — originality — imagination — courage — adaptability to changes

1	2	3	4	5
Poor	Fair	Good	Very Good	Excellent

4 JUDGEMENT — ability to size up a problem or situation and reach a sound conclusion, after consideration of all the facts — ability to make decisions which reflect sound judgement and are timely

1	2	3	4	5
Poor	Fair	Good	Very Good	Excellent

5 DEPENDABILITY — following instructions — promptness in getting the work done and meeting schedules

1	2	3	4	5
Poor	Fair	Good	Very Good	Excellent

6 PLANNING ability to plan, direct tasks and carry them out systematically

1	2	3	4	5
Poor	Fair	Good	Very Good	Excellent

7 CO-OPERATIVENESS teamwork − attitude towards others − relations with others − open-mindedness − receptivity to new ideas or changes

1	2	3	4	5
Poor	Fair	Good	Very Good	Excellent

8 CONSTRUCTIVE INFLUENCE ON OTHERS articulateness − ability to convey ideas − persuasiveness

1	2	3	4	5
Poor	Fair	Good	Very Good	Excellent

9 PERSONAL CHARACTERISTICS loyalty − integrity − self-control − temperament

1	2	3	4	5
Poor	Fair	Good	Very Good	Excellent

Section B (Use Section B when evaluating performance of team members responsible for supervising others.)

10 TEAM PERFORMANCE

(a) quality of work or service performed by the team

1	2	3	4	5
Poor	Fair	Good	Very Good	Excellent

(b) quantity or volume of work or service provided by the team

1	2	3	4	5
Poor	Fair	Good	Very Good	Excellent

(c) efficiency − economy in operations − prevention of waste of material, time and equipment − accident record of team

1	2	3	4	5
Poor	Fair	Good	Very Good	Excellent

11 SUPERVISION AND LEADERSHIP

(a)   delegation of responsibilities and authority

1	2	3	4	5
Poor	Fair	Good	Very Good	Excellent

(b)   selecting, organising, training and developing the team

1	2	3	4	5
Poor	Fair	Good	Very Good	Excellent

(c)   relationship with team − ability to develop a harmonious and effective team, reduction of team turnover, absence and lateness

1	2	3	4	5
Poor	Fair	Good	Very Good	Excellent

(d)   good housekeeping − care and orderliness of department or section and equipment

1	2	3	4	5
Poor	Fair	Good	Very Good	Excellent

Section C

Considering all aspects of the member − performance, personal qualities, abilities, application to the job − what are the member's −

12 Outstanding abilities or gifts?

_____

_____

13 Areas requiring improvement or hindering performance?

_____

_____

14 What plans have you made to develop these gifts and performance?

_____

_____

And for the Churches?

It is interesting to note that the principles of evaluation are to be found long before the Industrial Revolution and the advent of 'modern' management. They can be found in the writings of the New and Old Testaments and are certainly implicit in the Ten Commandments. Here is an example of a structured self-evaluation approach being used by some 'spiritually' oriented teams. Even though you may not be interested in the spiritual dimension, this approach shows that it is possible to attempt to assess the more subjective aspects of our nature.

Place a tick against the most appropriate description of yourself

1 *Spiritual Life*

(a) The life of holiness
- Little spiritual energy or understanding
- Some progress in spiritual awareness
- Seeks spiritual maturity and a pure life
- Definite growth in grace
- Sensitive and obedient to the Spirit

(b) Prayer and the regular use of the means of grace
- No regular prayer life; no planned Bible study
- Superficial praying; little Bible study
- Regular prayer pattern and Bible study
- Prayer life well established, constant study of Scripture
- Outstanding prayer life and spiritual understanding of Scripture

189

2 *Relationships*

(a) Love and concern for
    people
                                — Aloof; little interest or love shown

— Spasmodic concern, usually for favourites

— Friendly; generally supportive and helping

— Very friendly; shows no favouritism; sympathetic and shows practical concern

— Shows vital, consistent concern, gives of self

(b) Soul-winning – discipling — Non-effective in Christian witness or development of new Christians

— Shows some desire, but little effectiveness

— Capacity for and desire to witness effectively and encourage converts

— Effective witness and encourager of converts

— Very effective in soul-winning and discipling

3 *Pastoral Ministry* — No interest in pastoral ministry, unable to communicate

— Limited shepherding skills

— Effective as shepherd

— Above average in pastoral skills, communicates well

— Outstanding in wisdom, skills and performance as pastor

Other Self-evaluation Approaches

In the self-evaluation approach, the team leader distributes some self-evaluation material to the team, and each member goes through the material answering the questions. This method has the advantages of being:

- less threatening
- confidential
- more easily administered, and
- less demanding on time.

It is a useful method to begin with. You can use or adapt the forms described earlier in this chapter.

A second approach is to conduct a team evaluation in which the whole team sits down and discusses its performance and the performances of the leader and the members. This, however, requires skill and a mature attitude among the membership. I do not recommend that you start with this model.

Summary

Evaluation is a good thing, but like all good things it can be abused. In the next chapter, we shall consider what you can do with the results of the evaluation to ensure that you avoid the pitfalls that accompany evaluation and development.

Before you leave this chapter, you should attempt to complete all the documents as they apply to *you* in your team. Pay particular attention to how you *feel* about the questions and the answers that you give. It is your awareness of how you feel that helps you transform experience into learning.

PART 5
Building on Your Experience

TRAINING for SUCCESS

Chapter 13

One of the greatest privileges of working with people is to be able to know and love them. Industry is today rediscovering the power of love to motivate people. In the international best-seller *A Passion for Excellence*, the writers note how great leaders and successful teams have a real and deep care for their work and their people.[1] The word 'love' used in the context of business teams is strange to many people, yet it has been the hall-mark of team development since the first century. For it was Jesus who gave this key to his disciples: 'all men will know that you are my disciples, if you love one another.'[2]

You need to have a vision for your team, since this gives you direction and hope; you need to have faith in your team, since this gives you confidence; but you also need to love your team, since this gives you the desire to seek the best for them — 'faith, hope and love. But the greatest of these is love.'[3] Love ensures that your team develops. If you love them, you will train them.

Trouble with Evaluation
We have seen how useful evaluation can be in helping a team

develop, but there are problems with evaluation. Done well, it contributes to personal and team growth. Done badly, it can cause loss of confidence and a breakdown in relationships. What troubles with evaluation can you expect and how can they be avoided? There are five main sources of problem, and we shall consider these in turn.

The Administration

If you adopt evaluation as a method for helping the development of your team, it will become one of the most significant events in the life of the group. Evaluation should therefore not be taken lightly. It needs to be well organised, thoroughly prepared for and well administered. If it is rushed, done in a disorganised way, its value in the eyes of the team will be diminished. The team leader must also be committed to it and show his commitment. The team takes its signals from the leader's example. If he shows that evaluation is important, then the team begins to view it in the same way.

The Method

One ever present problem with evaluation is the difficulty of maintaining consistency between evaluation sessions. This is less likely to be an issue if each evaluation session is allowed plenty of time and the sessions are all spread over a short period — say a maximum of two weeks.

Within the evaluation meeting itself a problem can arise if the method of evaluation causes the discussion to be imbalanced. All major points have to be dealt with in a balanced way. I usually think of this in terms of a star — eight points need to be high-lighted:

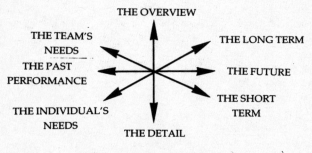

Balancing the Discussion

The Interview

You can take a number of precautions to ensure that the interview does not have problems built into it. First, make sure that you are well prepared and that all the paperwork is completed and to hand. Second, no interruptions: make sure that you are not disturbed − divert the phone; put notices on the doors. A surgeon does not stop to take casual calls in the middle of an operation, and evaluation is no less critical.

The Attitudes

Perhaps the most difficult problem to overcome is our prejudice. Bias for or against a team member undercuts our comments and the help that we offer. Avoid the 'halo' effect which surrounds the team member who can do nothing wrong and the converse 'cloven-hoof' syndrome in which the person can do nothing right! Check others' perceptions of the team member who is either 'very good' or 'very bad'.

Steer clear of negotiation − you are not setting out to strike bargains, make deals, bribe or win arguments. Nor are you there to settle scores: 'I've been waiting for six months to say this!' These are not the attitudes of love.

The Behaviours

Be aware not only of what you intend to do and say, but of what you actually do and say. Watch out for:

Avoidance	− backing off from the hard things which should be said, or from the good things
Aggression	− attacking the member or the leader as a means of defence
Threats	− coercing the member into accepting a situation or task
Non-verbal inconsistencies	for example, saying, 'Yes, I'm listening', − while you complete 5 down on the crossword!
Escapism	− promising anything and everything in order to keep the session smooth, then being unable to deliver or follow through on your commitments.

Despite the pitfalls associated with evaluation, its capacity to help the team members develop is such that you should be prepared to face the risks. But the evaluation session is only the beginning of the development process.

Follow up

Built into the planning chart I recommended you use − for any action arising from evaluation − is a review date (see page 183). This is to ensure that the leader and the member check progress regularly. The team leader should arrange to have one-to-one sessions with each member of the team on a regular basis throughout the year. A year is a long time to wait to express your case, your concern and your appreciation for someone as close as a team member, so spend time with each person: lunch together, shop together, walk together, relax together. Be committed to the success of the other − be a coach, a door-opener, a corrector, an encourager, a friend and a guide.

The Spirit of Being a Leader

All the members of your team are unique. Committed to their success and to discovering their potential, you may see them develop way beyond your own capabilities. If you love them, then their increase can only give you satisfaction. This is particularly true for younger members of the team − the ugly ducklings of this world − who have a great future before them, but who are so ungainly and unskilled that they create problems wherever they go!

Ugly ducklings are a team leader's delight. When a coach comes across future stars, he or she looks not to what the young untutored protégés are, but to what they can become. If you have any potential 'swans' in your team, here is what you should do:

1 Get alongside them.
2 Help them to discover and develop their gifts.
3 Help them to recognise their potential.
4 Help them to cope with the fact that really gifted people *are* unusual. Show them that you value them.
5 Teach them to understand themselves and others, so that they can be more effective in influencing situations, for too often the rising star is abrasive, insensitive and clumsy in relationships.
6 Teach them what you know about people and about teams. One thing television has done is to create a new breed of prima donnas in sport, whose sensitivity is zero and whose self-centredness is 100%. Unfortunately, these social 'pigmies' are being held up as the heroes and models for the generation that will be tomorrow's leaders.

Barriers to Giving Help

Obviously, to be a good leader requires you to develop skills in helping others. But giving help is not easy; it does not come naturally to most of us. Consider the following barriers:

1 Most of us *like to give advice*. It makes us feel important, but we are then in danger of satisfying our needs, not the needs of those with whom we are dealing. 'Give every man thine ear, but few thy voice' was the counsel of Shakespeare's Polonius to his son.[4] The adviser must first be a listener.

2 Often in our desire to help we may *argue*, or try to persuade, and the team member may become defensive or obstructive. We then resent those we are trying to help rejecting our 'wise' counsel. Be gentle with others; treat your team as tender plants − nurture them with care.

3 We may *over-praise*. This can confuse the situation. The team member must be able to see his limitations. Being supportive does not always mean praising. It means creating an atmosphere in which the team member can admit his faults and fears and know that you will *listen* and understand − not necessarily approve − and be willing to advise in a manner that best meets the need of the individual and the team.

4 Then there is the temptation to *deny* the team member's feelings: 'You don't really mean that'; 'You have no reason to feel that way'; 'Everybody has problems like that'. You may respond in this way because you are embarrassed or do not know how to cope with the member's problem. If that is true, say so. Then work out a joint strategy to get help.

5 Watch out for the temptation to tear down his *defence mechanisms*. They exist for a reason and must be treated with respect until such time as you fully understand the nature and purpose of the defence.

6 To avoid hurting her feelings, we *change the subject* − or worse, to avoid our *own* embarrassment, we change the subject.

7 Everyone loves to play the *psycho-analyst*: 'You do that because your mother always . . .'.

8 Our need to establish and identify with the team member causes us to *agree vigorously*. This binds him to what he has just said and makes further development difficult.

Helping is a skilled profession. Do not undervalue it!

Barriers to Receiving Help

Think now for a moment about being on the receiving end of advice.

1 Sometimes it is *hard to admit* our difficulties to ourselves, let alone to others.
2 We may be *afraid of what the other person thinks of us*, so we hide our problems.
3 We may wonder *if we can really trust* the other person, especially if we are in a club or church or a similarly close-knit situation where our standing with friends and colleagues might be affected.
4 We may *fear being dependent*, especially if we are proud of our independence.
5 We may be *looking for someone to be dependent on* – this will not help us, although it might make us feel better.
6 We may be *looking for sympathy and support*, rather than help in seeing our difficulty more clearly.
7 We may feel *our problem is so unique* that no one could ever understand it, and certainly not an outsider. Conversely, we may feel that it is *too trivial* to seek help.

Do you find it easier to give help than to ask for it?

Giving Your Team Feed-back

The purpose of feed-back is to provide information to a person or the group about behaviour, or performance or relationships.

If feed-back is to be useful, it must be given sensitively – a difficult task, particularly if the comments are negative. Here then are some guide-lines about giving feed-back. The key to making the choice of approach is the degree of trust between the people concerned.

1 Be specific. Say precisely what it was the person did which was good or bad. Do not generalise, eg 'Oh, you are always creating problems', or 'I think you are a great guy.'
2 Be constructive. Emphasise what and how something should be done.
3 Be responsive. If someone asks for feed-back, give it.
4 Be honest. Do not beat about the bush or avoid the problem.
5 Be balanced. Give positive with the negative.

In *Giving and Receiving Criticism*, the writer offers some help:

Solomon in his wisdom has reminded us that there is a time for all things. Criticism certainly needs to be timely, especially personal criticism. Personal criticism should never be given in front of others . . .

Don't use criticism as a method of rebuttal in an argument.

Don't criticise the person. Criticise the *action*.

Don't criticise in anger. You will usually over-react.

Get all the facts. Don't be drawn into a quick response because someone else has given you an emotionally charged account of a situation. There are always two sides − at least! On the other hand, criticise as soon as possible after the mistake has been made. Make sure that you have thought about what would have been the correct procedure before criticising the wrong one.

This suggests having planned times for a critique, times when the performance of the individual or team can be evaluated against agreed performance. Agreed performance should be based on what is to be done and on how to do it.[5]

How Good Are Your Team-development Skills?

This is a small checklist to assess your own attitude and practices towards developing others by means of coaching. Based on the work of Mike Woodcock, it also gives valuable pointers to the skills and behaviour required for good team development.[6]

How To Do It

(a) Complete the following five questions honestly by selecting one answer to each question. Place a circle around the letter which precedes the statement which best describes your approach in your team.

(b) Check your score using the score table.

1   Do you devote at least two hours of your time to coaching individuals in your team each month?
   (a)   Rarely
   (b)   Occasionally
   (c)   Usually
   (d)   Always
2   Do you:
   (a)   plan specific 'coaching assignments' or learning opportunities for each member of your team?
   (b)   keep an eye open for situations you can use for coaching purposes?
   (c)   let your team learn by the experiences which come their way in the normal course of business?
   (d)   consciously create coaching situations − even at the expense of some immediate priorities?

200

3   Who does most of your work when you are absent from the team?
    (a)   Someone always picks up the urgent things.
    (b)   My superior.
    (c)   The team takes over.
    (d)   Nobody. If the job is to be done properly, only I can do it — so I tackle it when I get back.

4   If the performance of a member of your team on a particular task clearly indicates a weakness in an area where you have special expertise, would your inclination be to:
    (a)   tell him exactly what he ought to have done and ensure that you supervise him closely next time?
    (b)   avoid delegating that type of work to him in the future?
    (c)   send him on a course or give him a book to read?
    (d)   get him to tackle another assignment of the same sort; ask him to report progress periodically, and review and discuss his problems as they arise?

5   If a member of your team comes and asks you what she should do about a problem which has arisen in connection with a task delegated to her, do you:
    (a)   tell her to come back in a couple of days, when you have the time to think about it?
    (b)   tell her politely that it is her job to find the answers, not yours?
    (c)   tell her what she should do?
    (d)   ask her what she would suggest should be done, and how?

Now transfer your answers to the table following.

Your Rating As a Team Developer

Your Score

	(a)	(b)	(c)	(d)	
1	1	2	3	4	_____
2	4	2	1	3	_____
3	3	1	4	2	_____
4	3	1	2	4	_____
5	3	2	1	4	_____

Now read off your rating:

5-10   You really need to work hard at improving your coaching skills.

11-16 You are within reach of being good at developing others.

17-20 You should be sharing your skill with others to help them become better coaches.

Part of the Job

The team leader has a vital role to play in the development of his team by operating as a coach or counsellor. Many team leaders accept this as sound common sense and have a genuine desire to play their part. For a variety of reasons – time or work pressures, disapproval from others, unwillingness to break new ground – this desire is often not converted into reality. Sometimes, team leaders feel they have not got the expertise to master yet another responsibility. But coaching is not the prerogative of the leader. Many leaders have been coached to success by a skilled member of their own team.

Essentially, coaching is the process of setting learning tasks, monitoring progress, reviewing and learning from experience. Each of these apparently simple steps requires just a little more explanation, which now follows.

Setting tasks As you set tasks, remember that each task should have a learning target and should be appropriate to the learner's ability, experience and development needs. Each task should also be capable of being monitored, with dead-lines, reports and explicit obligations to keep you informed.

Monitoring progress Meet regularly to discuss progress. Try to avoid providing answers (if you know them); let the learner find out for himself. Ask questions such as: 'What do *you* think?' or 'What would *you* propose?'.

Reviewing and learning While the tasks are in progress, as well as when they are complete, carry out a thorough review, by asking: 'Why did this work well?' 'How could we improve even more?' 'What went wrong?' 'How could it have been avoided?' 'What should we do next time?'

To be a good coach is to have the skills of the effective leader:

– to be able to listen carefully

– to support the learner at all times

– to help the learner analyse his own shortcomings and strengths

     – to set clear and attainable targets/objectives
     – to be aware of the feelings and needs of others.

Plan to improve your coaching by completing the action plan for coaching. This form will help ensure that you get into action on coaching. Complete one sheet for each member of your team.

Action Plan for Coaching

Team Member's name_____

1   Opportunites: What change do you want this person to achieve?

_____

_____

2   Targets: How will you know when the change is accomplished?

_____

_____

3   Timing: How long will this change take until completion?

_____

_____

4   Tactics: What specific activities/methods will you use to encourage the team member to change?

_____

_____

5   Monitoring: How and when will you monitor progress?

_____

_____

Check the following:
(a) Are the aims of the coaching important to you and the team member?
(b) Do the proposed methods offer a reasonable chance of success?
(c) Have you adequate resources to carry out the plan?

Remember You Too Are Fallible

Herewith, a short course in human relations which I came across framed on a senior manager's office wall. You will find it helpful as you try to develop your team.

The six most important words:

'I ADMIT I MADE A MISTAKE'.

The five most important words:

'YOU DID A GOOD JOB'.

The four most important words:

'WHAT IS YOUR OPINION'.

The three most important words:

'IF YOU PLEASE'.

The two most important words:

'THANK YOU'.

The one most important word:

'WE'.

The least important word:

'I'.

CONFLICT in GROUPS

Chapter 14

No book on people working with people would be complete without a consideration of conflict and how it may be resolved. First, let me say that not all conflict is bad. Conflict may be necessary for the team's survival if it is threatened from without or within. But any prolonged conflict is undesirable, since it places stress on individuals and on relationships.

No Escape

Conflict is a feature of our world, as is the search for peace. Nations come together in treaties, pacts and organisations in attempts to keep peace. We have the United Nations, NATO, the Warsaw Pact, the United Arab Republic, the Organisation of African States, peace-keeping forces, shuttle diplomacy and groups of 'eminent persons' — and still the world is wracked by conflict.

It is therefore unrealistic to expect that your team can escape its own pain. But here lies the difference: *outside* the team, the world expects conflict and can usually deal quickly with it; *within* the team, conflict often stuns the group into inaction! For example, the Security Council of the United Nations first met in

1946 and is designed to function continuously. Lord Caradon, the former permanent representative of the United Kingdom to the United Nations, states that: 'The existence of a small council with world-wide responsibilities and representation, wielding effective powers, and able to meet at few hours' notice, is surely one of the most hopeful developments of modern times.'[1]

Has someone in your team permanent responsibility and power to deal with conflict? The need for such a role in a group was identified as long ago as 1948. The role was described as the 'Harmoniser', yet I have come across very few teams who recognise the need for a peace-maker, despite their conflicts.[2]

Sources of Conflict

Conflict arises because someone wants what he cannot have. This simple observation comes from the first century AD and in my view has not been bettered.[3] Within the team, there are a number of objects at which that 'want' may be directed, and it is interesting to note that the list is almost the same as that which causes conflict to arise between nations:

- territorial conflicts − 'I want part, or all, of your job'
- border conflicts − 'That's my job!'
- resource conflicts − 'I'm using the car tonight!'
- ethnic conflicts − 'You're different!'
- influence conflicts − 'They won't listen to you!'
- ideological conflicts[4] − 'You're wrong!'

To this list we need only add 'personality-based conflicts' and we have covered 99% of the sources of conflict in a team.

Territorial conflicts in the group setting relate to competition for roles or responsibilities. I want to be chairman or to be given responsibility for the next project − so do you. You think you can do my job better than I can, and make attempts to take over my work. The conflict may be based on real, objective data. I *do* want your job as treasurer and *I am* determined to show up your shortcomings and inadequacies at every opportunity. Or, you may only *think* I want your job as treasurer and that every comment that I make about the quality of your work is a direct attack on your position. In fact, all I am trying to do is to improve your performance and strengthen your position as treasurer − I am just not doing it very well! Real or imagined, conflict has developed.

Border conflicts in teams arise when the roles and responsibilities

206

of team members are not clear. Overlap occurs between your role and my role, and where our boundaries touch there is confusion, friction and conflict. I think I am responsible for communication with the world outside the group, but as secretary you have the responsibility for the minutes, agenda and annual reports. I want to vet these, but you see them as your sole responsibility. It is not that I want your job or you mine, it is simply that we are not clear where our boundaries lie.

Resource conflict In the world it is oil or fish; in the team it is usually time or money. The team has a limited budget; it can only purchase one major piece of equipment this year – you want a photocopier, I want a projector. We want what we cannot have! Time is a more subtle source of conflict. It may be that I talk too much in the team and do not give you enough time to present your ideas and proposals.

Ethnic conflicts are one of the major problems facing the world today. We carry our prejudices into all situations, often without being aware of them. We discriminate. We try to put others 'in their place' – below us, of course!

Influence as a source of conflict is not easily recognised. You want to be the confidante of the team leader – so do I! You're only a woman! We tend to recruit in our own image: male or female, graduate or non-graduate, black or white.

Ideological conflicts cover a wide area and include religious prejudice and political differences. We value people who hold similar attitudes and priorities – and we get into conflict with those who differ from us.

Personality-based conflicts come from within. 'The hostile person is one who has developed feelings of insecurity and now tries to protect his weak self-concept by attacking others.'[5] Conflicts can also arise due to thinking patterns; for example, highly evaluative, critical thinkers often get into conflict with creative thinkers, since the evaluator can see no value in the 'way-out' ideas of the innovator, while the creative thinker will feel under constant pressure and attack by the critical thinker. Yet both are needed in the group.

What sources of conflict do you experience in your team? Whatever the source of conflict, we need to deal with it promptly and effectively, for unchecked conflict can damage or even destroy the team.

Outcomes of Conflict

Conflict can escalate into all-out war or can be transformed into peace. But there is peace and peace!

There is the peace that descends on the battle-field when the last combatants on both sides have destroyed themselves. This is the peace of mutual destruction. Never again will the committee room ring to the shouts and arguments of the team — because there is no team. Unable to hold itself together, it destroys itself and 'peace' is restored — but at what a cost? All across our land there stand monuments to the effectiveness of the final solution: factory gates stand locked with rusting padlocks, tributes to the effectiveness and commitment of unions and management who fought to the end to hold their positions, only to lose everything in the conflict. Churches too stand empty, their spires still pointing in the one direction which could have united the opposing parties, but no one could find common ground; the church was split and everyone lost.

There is also the peace that comes from the destruction of the 'enemy'. By overwhelming force, logic, power or prejudice, we gain the victory and vanquish the foe. So the team can get back to the real business of team-work — one or two members short perhaps, and with a few scars round the table — but then, might is right and we have made the choice. In 'victory' we have, however, lost something — the trust of the team — for now around the table are those who witnessed our ruthless treatment of the opposition. When will we next exercise that power? Who will be next to be at the wrong end of our big guns? A win and lose outcome is, in the end, an outcome of complete loss.

Finally, there is the peace of compromise. I give a bit, you give a bit — for the sake of the team — and we are all happy. Or are we? Have we not all lost? I resent having to give my bit and you resent having had to give your bit. We can live with our resentment for the moment, but our time will come!

Resolving Conflict

There are a number of approaches you can adopt towards conflict and its resolution. The main strategies open to you are discussed here:

- Submission
- Collaboration
- Avoidance
- Non-co-operation
- Competition
- *Pax Romana*
- Confrontation
- Joint problem solving

Submission requires one party to surrender its position and interests. This method is often used when the conflict is between people of different rank or status in the team. The more powerful person forces his views on the weaker member. It may also be a method adopted by someone who has more interest in the group's unity than in the 'rightness' of his own position. Submission is not a sound basis for building harmony in the team. It should not be encouraged. Differences and conflict should be worked through and solutions agreed, not imposed. Submission requires you to give up your visions and targets, and take on those of others.

Collaboration 'If you cannot beat them, then join them' is a philosophy widely used in conflict. Once again, as in the case of submission, the 'solution' focuses on the difference in strengths of the parties involved. Collaboration involves compromise, but the major difference between collaboration and submission is that you have not given up your own visions and targets. Collaboration gives you a respite from the conflict — time to regroup, time to grow stronger, time in which to subvert the opposition. Collaboration is often the false peace — the peace which is no more than preparation for renewed conflict.

Avoidance is quite an effective way to deal with conflict, provided the opposition will let you! 'I'm not going to argue with you', says the hard pressed father. 'Just do as I tell you!' In teams it may be difficult to adopt an avoidance strategy. You can absent yourself from meetings; you can refuse to rise to challenges or respond to attacks. The old adage 'He who fights and runs away, lives to fight another day' does not fit here. If you use avoidance techniques, then you are faced with 'He who doesn't fight but runs away lives to keep on running!' Avoidance is a self-indulgence which the team can well do without, because it strikes at the very heart of team spirit.

Non-co-operation is the tactic of the subversive. 'OK, I'll go along with you.' But (heavy aside) 'I'll scream and kick all the way!' This is not a resolution, it is an agreement to exchange the pitched battle for an endless series of skirmishes, ambushes and surprise attacks.

Competition 'May the best man win' is a technique for resolving conflict often adopted by a weak leader. Unable to reach peace by any other method, in effect everyone stands back and lets the adversaries slog it out toe to toe. The group can then gather round and pick up the pieces. There is no place for competition within the team. Conflict cannot be solved in this way if the team is to remain whole.

Pax Romana One method used widely for the containment of conflict is the enforced peace. The nation of Lebanon and its capital Beirut has much experience of this – Israel, Syria, UN forces and militia men of all descriptions. In response to the Iran/Iraq war, the Gulf States have taken a number of measures to strengthen regional security and contain the conflict. They have established new pacts, begun to establish a mobile reactionary force, set up a joint air defence system and a combined Gulf naval patrol. They intend to maintain peace at any cost and by all force![6] *Pax Romana* held the conquered nations together in the turbulent first century, but it was a forced peace. Within the team, a strong chairman can contain conflict, but he must do more than contain it. He must use the peace to work through the roots of the conflict and resolve it permanently. Otherwise time weakens his grip, and as his power wanes, so war will wax.

Open confrontation is often the best way to resolve conflict, although there needs to be some mechanism to ensure that neither one nor both parties receive permanent damage. This can be done by use of a third party as a reconciliator or arbitrator.

Joint Problem Solving

Clearly, the foregoing approaches to the 'resolution' of conflict – although all common – are in some way or other unsatisfactory. As long as one party believes it can win, no resolution is possible other than victory, and as we have seen, victory means a loss for both sides. Clearly, a different approach is needed, an approach in which both parties recognise that they *both* have a problem and that they are *both* losing. In the very readable book *Getting to Yes*, the authors describe a joint problem-solving approach to conflict resolution. This approach emphasises the need for a focus on the future and a creative solution based on agreed criteria for success.[7]

The table overleaf compares some of the features of three of the approaches that we have considered.

It is clear that the joint problem-solving approach offers both sides a way forward with honour. But what if the parties won't join together?

Using a Mediator

A third party is often useful in resolving long-standing conflict, but the choice of mediator is important. Here are some guide-lines; the mediator must –

— be acceptable to both parties

FEATURES	APPROACHES		
	Confrontation	Collaboration	Joint Problem Solving
The parties are:	Adversaries	Friends	Joint Problem Solvers
The target is:	Victory	Agreement	A wise outcome
Attitudes to relationship:	Demands concessions as a precondition	Encourages concessions as an entry fee	Separates relationships from the problem
The values are to be:	Hard on people and hard on the problem	Soft on people and soft on the problem	Soft on people, but hard on the problem
The positions are:	To dig in	To change readily	Not important; the future is the focus
Offers:	Threats	Compromises	A creative solution
Outcomes:	I win, you lose	You win, I lose	You win, I win
Priorities:	Insist on my position	Insist on agreement	Insist on objective criteria

- have authority with both parties
- be wise and responsible
- be detached from the conflict, so that he may take an objective view
- be able to understand the positions, feelings and objectives of both parties
- be skilled at problem analysis and in interpersonal relationships.

The process will soon break down if either party detects that the mediator does not meet any one of these criteria.

Inter-group Conflict

Before I conclude this chapter on conflict, let us consider conflict between groups. What happens when your team comes into conflict with another team? This is always a danger for the very strong team.

Do not forget that in conflict your group's experience is likely to be similar to the experience of the other group. Feelings rise in both teams, and the following effects become noticeable.

1   Each group pulls in closer together as a team and begins to view the other group as 'the enemy'. At the same time, group loyalty increases. Suddenly we become a 'good group' and we forget our internal difficulties.
2   Each group begins to see only the best in itself and the worst in the other group. Filters or screens are put up for incoming information, so that what we see and hear of the other team confirms our worst fears.
3   Each group feels that it owns, and must guard, certain territory (its rooms, responsibilities or budget, etc). Any move by the other group is seen as threatening our position.
4   Each group demands more conformity from its members and accepts more control from its leaders. This may lead to changes in leadership style or even in the leadership itself.
5   The group atmosphere changes; it becomes more serious and more business-like.
6   Each group becomes more structured, alert, and organised.

While all this is going on within each group, changes are taking place in relation to the other team:

1   Members become hostile towards the other group, snubbing them and spreading rumours.
2   Bad stereotypes form of the other group, based on the worst assumptions about their motives.
3   Interaction and communication decrease: the groups do not want to see the other point of view or position and do not understand the opposition's thinking.
4   Members do not listen to the 'adversary'; they hear only what supports their own position; they may even attack points of the adversary's position which are supported by their own group's position.
5   Members mistrust the other group (and its representatives); they see them as sneaky and unfair. There is a strong emphasis on politics, rather than solving the problem on its merits.

Effects like these are familiar enough; we can see them whenever groups – departments of a church, competing organisations, cities, parts of a nation, or nations themselves – must interact to solve some common problem. And many of these effects also occur between individuals when they see their relationship with others as competitive. Competition leads to hostility, suspicion, and misunderstanding.

We are educated in a competitive system; we work in competitive systems; we are rewarded by being better than others. Much of our training is about how to compete. But what we need now is training on how to co-operate, training on how to resolve conflict — anyone can *start* a war!

Developing Co-operation Between Groups

How can the negative effects described above be reduced so that good problem solving can be maintained and conflict held at an acceptable level? Conflict *can* lead to creative tension out of which come new joint initiatives. Three ways of developing co-operation are described below.

Creating the Common Vision

Finding an overriding vision or target — one which both (or all) groups accept as essential and realistic. Thus 'Win-Lose' becomes changed to 'Win-Win'. Such a target is often a 'higher-order', more inclusive target. If one group wants X, and the other wants Y, and each sees the other as preventing what they want, then the way out could be: 'How can we set things up so we *both* get what we want?' This is not easy (but does work). One example was when Russian and Western nuclear experts joined forces in the face of the common threat of the Chernobyl disaster.

Creating a Third Group

Creating a third group that contains respected members from each group (not representatives as such) is often useful. However, the task on which they work must be unrelated to the win-lose issue dividing the groups. Having to work together produces new norms and more positive attitudes which the respected members then carry back to their own groups and help to spread. This can be a slow process, but may work well when the conflict has been long-standing.

The Confrontation Meeting

Inter-group 'maintenance' operations have also proved helpful, though these require that the groups genuinely wish to improve their relationship. In this procedure, representatives of each group meet to discuss the perceptions they have of the other group and get them clarified. One approach is for each group to produce four flip charts for their representatives to share with the other group. The flip charts could contain statements under the following headings:

(a) How we see ourselves

(b) How we think the other group sees us

(c) How we see the other group

(d) How we think the other group sees themselves.

Inter-group problem solving is a highly skilled — or gifted — activity. Although it is not the topic of this text, it is necessary to high-light the issue, since as any one group develops, it runs the risk of becoming the target for jealousy and criticism.

Remember, real co-operation is not possible as long as one group thinks it can WIN!

A Basis for Reconciliation

Whatever method you adopt to attempt to resolve conflict, whatever its source, it seems that there are four basic principles that must form the basis for reconciliation. These are:

— equality

— mutual respect

— factual accuracy, and

— concensus.

These principles lie not only at the heart of all conflict resolution; they lie at the heart of team building. For the team is based on the fact that all men are equal in the sight of God and that no man is complete in isolation. In teamwork and in conflict resolution, each member must have equal rights of expression, consideration, support and love. From this principle flows the second — of mutual respect: I may not agree with your view, but I assume that you hold that view sincerely and honestly. I also assume that you have a genuine desire to reach agreement and to solve the problem in a way that respects my position and feelings. Although my feelings are important, it is the real, objective, factual world that will help us resolve our differences and work together as a team. The basis of our agreements and our reconciliation will be open to examination and not based on sentimentality or subjective emotion. Factual accuracy — the truth in love — will be one of the objective criteria we insist upon. And finally, because of the first three principles, we will operate by concensus — not by vote. We will agree to agree, for the penalties of disagreement are such that we cannot afford to rest until all is resolved.

In the concluding lines of his book *Conflicts*, Edward de Bono writes:

> The costs of conflicts can be so enormous that even some improvement must be worth having. We can expect considerable improvement once we realise the inadequacy of our usual conflict thinking.
>
> There can be no more important matter for the future of the world than conflict resolution.[8]

TEAM SPIRIT

Chapter 15

And so we reach the final chapter. You have demonstrated your commitment and motivation. You have identified the skills you need — and have begun, I hope, to develop them, apply them, evaluate your performance, and build on your experience.

What more do you need? Two things. The first is time, time to learn, time to grow, time to become what you can be — a good leader and a good member. And the second thing? The second requirement is team spirit.

Team Spirit

Though I understand all the words used in team building,
And though I can appreciate different cultures,
If I do not know the meaning of team spirit,
My words are hollow and carry no weight.

And though I am a visionary and can set objectives,
Solve problems and analyse situations;
And though I believe in myself and can achieve great things,
If I am not motivated by team spirit, my actions will come to
    nothing.

And though I spend all my time and resources on behalf of the
    group
And burn myself out in the course of my effort,
If I do these things outside all the spirit of the team, no one
    benefits.

Team spirit is characterised by patience, acceptance and humil-
    ity;
It is not associated with force, imposition, provocation or treach-
    ery.
Team spirit is concerned with true facts and feelings.
Its concern with the truth enables the team to cope with difficul-
    ties
And to maintain the team vision in the face of the strongest
    opposition.

Team spirit will see the team through every set-back.
The team may fail to meet its objectives;
Communication may break down,
And the team may fail to practise its skills and gifts.
All this might happen, for no team is perfect,
And like children with so much still to learn, we all struggle for
    understanding.
But with team spirit we can learn to grow together
And as we learn we can put behind us the immature behaviour.

At the moment our vision of what our team might be is unclear
But as we move forward together, the possibilities will open
    before us.
A team depends on commitment, motivation and team spirit,
No team can survive without these three, but team spirit is the
    ultimate objective.
Based on the writings of St Paul. For 'team spirit' also read 'love'.

Notes

Introduction
[1] Alex De Tocqueville, quoted in Edward Dayton, *What Ever Happened to Commitment* (Zondervan: Grand Rapids, 1984), p 143.
[2] Cheryl Forbes, *The Religion of Power* (MARC Europe: London, 1986), p 116.
[3] *ibid*, p 84.
[4] Professor David McClelland, 'Power Is the Great Motivator', *Harvard Business Review* (March 1976).
[5] Matthew 5:14 and 13.
[6] Gaius Petronius, quoted in Hastings, Bixby and Chaudhry-Lawton, *The Superteam Solution* (Gower: Aldershot, 1986), p 17.
[7] Dayton, *op cit*, p 130.
[8] II Timothy 3:7.
[9] Thomas Peters and Robert Waterman, Jnr, *In Search of Excellence* (Harper & Row: New York), p 126.
[10] Kenneth Blanchard and Spencer Johnson, *The One Minute Manager* (Collins: London 1986), p 16.

Chapter 1
[1] Meredith Belbin, *Management Teams* (Heinemann: London, 1981).
[2] Video Arts Films, London.
[3] Matthew 4:3.
[4] Matthew 3:17.
[5] Matthew 12:50.
[6] Matthew 4:4.
[7] Matthew 4:10.
[8] Matthew 4:19.
[9] Matthew 19:21.
[10] Luke 9:10.
[11] David Cormack, *Seconds Away!* (MARC Europe: London, 1986), p 110.
[12] Matthew 17:22.
[13] Matthew 25:21.
[14] Matthew 16:23.
[15] Matthew 16:15.
[16] Matthew 13:10.
[17] John 21:15 ff.
[18] Cormack, *op cit*, pp 49-54.
[19] *New Collins Concise English Dictionary*, p 1200.

Chapter 2
[1] Peter Wagner, *Leading Your Church to Growth* (MARC Europe: London, 1985), p 100.
[2] Peter Tannenbaum and Warren Schmidt, *Harvard Business Review* Vol 36, no 2 (March 1958).
[3] Hastings, Bixby and Chaudhry-Lawton, *op cit*, p 95.

4 John Adair, *Effective Team Building* (Gower: Aldershot, 1986), p 39.

Chapter 3
1 Abraham Maslow, *Motivation and Personality* (Harper and Row: New York, 1954).
2 Mike Woodcock and Dave Francis, *The Unblocked Manager* (Gower: Adlershot, 1985).
3 Matthew 25:21.
4 Matthew 16:17.
5 John 21:15.
6 John 21:16.
7 Luke 10:42.

Chapter 4
1 Adair, *op cit*, pp 39-46.
2 Hastings, Bixby, and Chaudhry-Lawton, *op cit*, p 95.
3 Cormack, *op cit*, p 94.
4 Matthew 17:1-9.
5 Charles Handy, *Organisations* (Pelican: London, 1985).

Chapter 5
1 Charles Handy, *Gods of Management* (Pan Books: London, 1985), pp 17-31.
2 I Corinthians 12:17-19.
3 Adair, *op cit*.
4 Hastings, Bixby, and Chaudhry-Lawton, *op cit*.
5 Mike Woodcock, *Team Development Manual* (Gower: Aldershot, 1979), p 3.
6 Geoffrey Mills, *On the Board* (Allen & Unwin: London, 1985).
7 Edward De Bono, *Lateral Thinking for Management* (Pelican Books: London, 1982).
8 Desmond Morris, *Manwatching* (Triad/Panther: London, 1978).
9 Pamela Ramsden, *Top Team Planning* (Assoc Business Programmes Ltd: London, 1973), p 34.
10 Gordon Wainwright, *Teach Yourself Body Language* (Hodder: London, 1985).
11 M Mayeroff, *On Caring* (Perennial Library, Harper and Row: New York, 1971), pp 41-42.
12 Gerard Egan, *The Skilled Helper* (Brooks/Cole: Monterey, California, 1975).
13 Cormack, *op cit*.

Chapter 6
1 Adair, *op cit*, p 121.
2 John 2:1-11.
3 Ephesians 4:16.
4 Adair, *op cit*, p 138.
5 Rosemary Sutcliffe, *Eagle of the Ninth* (Oxford University Press, 1954).

Chapter 7
1 Dayton, *op cit*, p 43.
2 John 21:3.
3 Chris Bonnington, *Everest the Hard Way* (Hodder & Stoughton: London, 1976).
4 Solomon in Proverbs 11:14.
5 De Bono, *op cit*, p 1.

Chapter 8
[1] Winston Fletcher, *Meetings, Meetings* (Coronet, Hodder & Stoughton: London, 1985), p 3.
[2] Edward Dayton and Ted Engstrom, *Strategy for Leadership* (MARC Europe: London, 1985), p 209.
[3] Mills, *op cit.*
[4] *ibid*, pp 65-70.
[5] *ibid*, pp 254-256.
[6] Chairman Mao Tsetung, *On Practice: Selected Works, Vol I* (Foreign Language Press: Peking, 1972), p 304.

Chapter 9
[1] John Hunt, *The Ascent of Everest* (Hodder & Stoughton: London, 1953), p 205.
[2] John Gardner, *The Anti-Leadership Vaccine* (Annual Report of the Carnegie Corporation: New York, 1965), p 12.
[3] Philip Greenslade, *Leadership* (Marshalls: Basingstoke, 1984), p 198.
[4] Matthew 4:19.
[5] I Thessalonians 1:6.
[6] Warren Bennis and Burt Nanus, *Leaders* (Harper & Row: New York, 1985), p 65.

Chapter 10
[1] Stephen Pile, *The Book of Heroic Failures* (Book Club Associates, 1980), p 17.
[2] Leo Tolstoy, *Anna Karenina* (Collins: London), p 1.
[3] I owe the insights of this section to Professor Gerry Harvey, *The Abilene Paradox* (Organisation Dynamics: Summer 1974), pp 63-80.

Chapter 12
[1] Cormack, *op cit*, p 79.

Chapter 13
[1] Tom Peters and Nancy Austin, *A Passion for Excellence* (Fontana: London, 1986).
[2] John 13:35.
[3] I Corinthians 13:13.
[4] William Shakespeare, *Hamlet* (Act I, Sc iii, l 68) in *William Shakespeare: The Complete Works* (Penguin: London, 1969).
[5] 'Giving and Receiving Criticism', *Christian Leadership Letter* (December 1978).
[6] Woodcock, *op cit*, pp 91-96.

Chapter 14
[1] Lord Caradon, *The Security Council as an Instrument of Peace in Multilateral Negotiations and Mediation*, A S Lall, editor (Pergamon Press: Oxford, 1985), p 4.
[2] Kenneth Banne and Paul Sleats, 'Functional Roles of Group Members', *Journal of Social Issues*, Vol 4, no 2 (1948): pp 41-49.
[3] James 4:2.
[4] Dr Falk Bomsdorf, *The Third World, Europe and Confidence Building Measures in Peace-keeping in the Third World* (Report No 20 of the International Peace Academy: New York, 1985), p 85.
[5] Clyde Narramore, *The Compact Encyclopedia of Psychological Problems* (Zondervan: Grand Rapids, 1966), p 162.
[6] Major Gen Indor Jit Rikhye, *Security Quest for Regional Co-operation* (Report No 22 of the International Peace Academy: New York, 1985), p 5.
[7] Roger Fisher and William Ury, *Getting to Yes* (Hutchinson: London, 1983).
[8] Edward De Bono, *Conflicts* (Harrap: London, 1985), p 196.

INDEX